AMERICAN COUNTRY BUILDING DESIGN

Rediscovered Plans for
19th-Century Farmhouses,
Cottages, Landscapes, Barns,
Carriage Houses & Outbuildings

Donald J. Berg

Sterling Publishing Co., Inc.
New York

Library of Congress Cataloging-in-Publication Data Available

2 4 6 8 10 9 7 5 3 1

Published in 2005 by Sterling Publishing Co., Inc.
387 Park Avenue South, New York, NY 10016
© 1997 by Donald J. Berg
Distributed in Canada by Sterling Publishing
c/o Canadian Manda Group, 165 Dufferin Street
Toronto, Ontario, Canada M6K 3H6
Distributed in Great Britain by Chrysalis Books Group PLC
The Chrysalis Building, Bramley Road, London W10 6SP, England
Distributed in Australia by Capricorn Link (Australia) Pty. Ltd.
P.O. Box 704, Windsor, NSW 2756, Australia

Sterling ISBN 1-4027-2357-1

Contents

Thanks

I'd like to thank my daughter Bethany for her help scanning and editing the old-time text, my son Christopher for taking time in his cross-country travels to photograph farms and my son Ted for enduring endless rides through the countryside. My friend Steve Rakeman found many of the farm journal articles and plans. The Durnan families shared photographs and records of their homes.

I'd like to thank the folks at the Museum of American Folk Art for their help and for allowing me to use their library. Joan Sandler invited me to speak at the museum and that forced me to organize my thoughts. Gerard Wertkin opened my eyes to some of the traditions behind the designs, and Lee Kogan was kind enough to offer valuable ideas and to guide me through the morass of research.

Most of all, I'd like to thank my wife, Christine, for her patience with my dawdling through this project, for her editing and proofreading, and for all the improvements that she suggested.

Samuel Sloan, Architect
Sloan's Homestead Architecture, 1866

Introduction

America's Eden is the picture-postcard scene of a white farmhouse, backed by red barns and a quilt of fields. It's our myth of a simpler, better time, when neighbors lived in harmony, when food was homegrown wholesome and when nature was pristine. It's the image of our anthems, a promised land to our politicians, and the stage set of Chevy ads. It's the place that freed slaves planned to build and that immigrant home rushers raced to. It's a pretty good myth because there is a bit of substance to it. Common American country buildings are fine symbols of our mix of cultures, of our dynamism, and of a wonderful neighborliness that we once had.

Like all of our country buildings, American farmhouses, barns and outbuildings grew from a blend of regional and old-world cultural building traditions, common customs and a barrage of printed images from urban architects and artists. The farmstead developed because of dramatic changes in the structure of American life and because country builders learned a new way to share ideas with each other.

The changes in our society in the first few decades of the 19th century were so fast and so sweeping that everyone was a Rip Van Winkle, napping as a colonial, with old-world ways, and waking as something very different. America became what it is in a catnap. The list of what we created or acquired is boggling: railroads; the whole West, from the Alleghenies to the Pacific; currency and banks; steamships; merchant fleets; factories and industry; countless books, newspapers and magazines; the telegraph; new religions and waves of revivals of the old ones; new citizens from all the world; technology that revolutionized farming and most other trades; and thousands of new towns and villages.

The changes were mirrored in our buildings. New types of structures like factories and tenements were invented. New versions of the old types were built and old buildings were renovated. New shapes were experimented with. We tried octagon houses and round barns. Concrete was reinvented and the new "balloon" frame, using easy-to-handle small boards, in place of heavy timbers, became popular. The White House and Capitol were completed, as were most of our statehouses and courthouses. These are still the sculptural symbols of our country. We gave up inefficient open fireplaces for iron stoves and boilers. We started preserving our common wood buildings with coats of paint. And country builders changed the way that they presented their designs. They started using a new language.

The new language was a graphic one. Plans, published in popular books and newspapers, first by architects and later by farmers and other country builders, allowed the quick spread of ideas. Less encumbered by the differences in language and dialect that isolated our regions, these sketches were recognizable by all. In 1830, if a New York architect suggested to a Midwest farmer that his house needed "umbrage," the farmer might take umbrage, or be confused. He might not be familiar, either, with other recently imported terms like "veranda" or "piazza" or with old regional ones like "stoop." On plan, or in a perspective sketch, he'd recognize a front porch for what it was.

Published plans directly reflected our country building boom. They became incredibly popular, spawning hundreds of books and monthly features in

Godey's Lady's Book, 1849

magazines as different as fashionable *Peterson's Magazine* and down-to-sod *Prairie Farmer. Godey's Lady's Book* published a monthly fashion plate with the latest trend in dresses and another plate with the trendiest home plan. Builders shared sketches of their successes through new trade journals like *Carpentry and Building.* Architects introduced villas from Europe. Farmers scribbled plans of the piggeries that worked well for them. Farm journals published designs of the best barns of each region. Aspiring architects and farm wives competed against each other in county fair contests for the best farmhouse designs. The architects expected to go on to fortune; the farm wives just wanted better kitchens. They all learned from each other, and together they created a new way of building.

Fortunately, we can learn from them too. Most of what they rendered remains. The record is a clear, graphic proof of the wonderful collision of cultures that built America. In the sampling on the following pages, you'll see arrogant urban architects humbled to adopt a new style to appeal to country builders. You'll also see plain farmers considering whether "Italianate" was better than "Gothic" just the way they considered Holsteins and Devons. You'll see building innovations on new Western homesteads and traditions from the old Eastern regions. But, most of all, you'll see a type of home that was shared, countrywide, by a large portion of our population, a type that can truly be called American.

Today we take our common country places for granted, but many of them are uncommonly beautiful. Covered bridges, spired churches, big barns, neat villages, and rambling farmhouses, all bold white and red, square and in order against the patchwork of fields and the green chaos of nature. American architects make pilgrimages to Europe to see castles, coliseums, and cathedrals. European architects come here to see our farms. The castles and cathedrals are stone; they will be there for centuries. Our heritage is wood; it's disappearing daily.

Henry David Thoreau wrote that he "traveled much in Concord"; he appreciated the common, nearby wonders that others overlooked. In this book we'll be traveling in all the Concords and Milfords and Springfields of America. I hope that it helps you appreciate them.

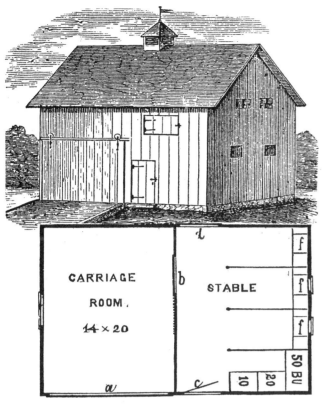

The American Agriculturist,
1880

About This Book

This book is about the plans that America was built from. Most of the text and drawings that appear on these pages are taken directly from 19th century manuscripts. Please forgive the quality of some of the reproductions and appreciate that they are from tattered, time-darkened paper. You'll notice that I've tried to let you hear different voices throughout the book.

> All of the text by 19th century authors is framed like this and set in this more ornate typeface.

I've tried to leave their text exactly as it was written, archaic phrases, strange punctuation and all. Where I've had to edit their words, it was just for brevity. Yesterday's Americans were very wordy. With that in mind, I've tried to keep my own comments to a minimum. Be warned that whatever you see in this simpler typeface is my own.

You'll see that, wherever I could, I credited the designs to individuals. In some cases those individuals are the authors of the source book, and not necessarily the building's designers. Some of the books that I used were compilations of previously published plans and credit was rarely given. You'll also see that outline type for their titles.

I use the term *architect* although that word was not as clearly defined as it is today. I tried to use that term to help you appreciate the difference between the high-style ideas of those people who supported themselves as building designers and the more common concepts of those who had other professions. In general I use the authors' own claims to the term architect, regardless of the level of their training. George Woodward, who started as a "horticulturist" seems to have become an architect through the process of publishing his plan books. Lewis Allen, who also published a plan book and numerous designs in farm journals, continued to consider himself a farmer.

Andrew Jackson Downing worked as a landscape designer and nurseryman while authoring his books, but, soon after, established an architectural practice with English architect Calvert Vaux. I consider him a professional because it seems that one of the purposes of his books was to establish himself as a designer for a future practice. Farm journal editor John J. Thomas, also a nurseryman, seems to have designed, published and built more buildings than Downing and many of the other professionals, but always wrote from the point of view of the farmer and country builder and never claimed to be anything else.

Historian Allen Nobel said, "Speculation plays a large part in the study of folk and vernacular buildings, and it is a large part of the fun of such a study." I've had to have a good deal of speculative fun with these labels, so please take none as gospel.

In general the "architects" lived in or near Eastern cities; were trained, apprenticed or self-educated in the arts; and were professional enough to support themselves either by designing buildings or by designing and publishing building books. Designers without that appellation seemed to support themselves doing something else and were generally from rural areas. Their building designs were a hobby, a one-time event, or as with farmers and farm journal editors, an adjunct to their work.

The time period that this book focuses on, from the 1830s through the early 1880s, coincides with the publication of most of the plan books that were aimed at country builders and, not coincidentally, with the settlement of the West, the homestead building boom, waves of immigration, and the creation of most our country villages and farmsteads. Plan books from this period tend to use woodcut illustrations and plans which were simple enough to encourage builders to make changes. Many of the original books that I used show pencil drawings of rearranged floor plans next to the originals. How and why country folk changed the plans is as fascinating as the original designs. The physical buildings that were inspired by these early plans usually mixed folk building traditions and community customs with the ideas that the authors presented.

By the late 1880s most new plan books were catalogs for the sale of architects' construction drawings and were aimed at a new, suburban construction boom. Illustrations in these later books were better because of the use of engraved metal plates and because the architects learned to spice their renderings with stylish people and backgrounds of elegant neighborhoods. Each image was an advertisement for a building plan. In the later books, the writing deteriorated as much as the illustrations improved. Where the earlier authors wrote eloquently and were very loquacious, the later ones wrote with the cryptic, chopped style that architects develop from the repeated chore of writing construction notes on drawings. Where Lewis Allen wrote three pages on the construction of cellars in his 1852 book *Rural Architecture,* George Palliser used just three words, "cellar by owner," in his 1883 *Model Homes* catalog.

Because the later books offered complete construction documents, with carefully drafted plans, details and specifications, their designs were less open to interpretation. These later designs were most often built exactly as drawn. From coast to coast, thousands of these suburban homes can still be found, looking just like their original designs. Plan book buildings, after 1885, tend to present the taste and talent of the individual architect rather than the collage of ideas that the earlier buildings show us.

I concentrated on the earlier books because their designs seemed to be pieces of the American collage.

This book grew out of another called *Country Patterns* and from my search for what was common to our common country buildings. I read an old farm-

er's letter in reaction to an 1849 published design for an "English Cottage." He asked, "Are we never to have any American Cottages?" and I wondered too. With all the styles that dot our landscape, what is American?

I searched through 134 different 19th century plan books and countless old magazines and saw over two thousand different building designs. Since the vast majority of yesterday's Americans were farmers, I also looked for plans published in farm journals and found hundreds more. I winnowed the designs by concentrating first on those designs labeled "American" in style and then the ones called "Farmhouse." In those designs I noticed little consistency in visual style but remarkably similar plan features. I then looked for other designs that had all or most of those same features.

As an architect, I came to this search prepared to find the architects who designed yesterday's countryside. Instead, I found farmers. The plans I culled precisely matched design criteria published by farm journals in articles like "General Rules for Building" in *The Register of Rural Affairs* of 1856. As you'll see, they are also similar to designs that won prizes at agricultural fairs.

There are very few designs in this book that present just what was commonly built. Traditional solutions were usually not published; everyone understood them already. I was often frustrated by notes like one in an 1858 issue of *The Register of Rural Affairs* that explained that an illustration wasn't provided because "the barn is built on the usual plan." Historian John Michael Vlatch said that the builders of the time "tended to negotiate cautiously between the often contradictory attractions of fashion and tradition." View these published designs as fashion and innovation and think of them morphed with simpler common structures to imagine what was actually built. Look for what the various designs have in common and you'll start to see what was commonly built.

There are wonderful works on the study of America's country buildings, books that I used to help understand what I was seeing in my old texts. You'll find many listed in the bibliography. You can think of this book as a farmhouse front porch: as your entrance to those more complete studies or just as a place to relax and enjoy a distant view.

Chapter 1

When Everything Changed

The common 17th and 18th century American homestead looked nothing like today's image of the farm. It was a weathered claptrap of gray stone and grayer wood. Animals roamed free; fields and gardens were fenced to keep them out. There was a bursting, small, all-purpose barn; scattered, rough outbuildings and a house that squeezed family life into tight, mixed-use rooms.

One main room would serve as kitchen, dining room, wash room, family room, farm manufactory and bedroom. If there was another room, it might be bedroom, pantry, parlor and storage. For its purpose, it was fine. Each year, the just-get-by farmer only needed to raise enough to eat well while allowing himself the time to "make land" or carve one more acre out of the wilderness. Virgin forest was almost worthless, but, cleared of trees and rocks, it was a farmer's guarantee

of a slightly easier future. Each cleared acre meant more land for planting or pasture and a larger legacy for his children. Subsistence was the primary goal. Improvements to buildings meant little and were usually ignored.

Although colonial America enjoyed a mix of ethnic cultures, few groups lived and built together. In general, the English settlers built colonial New England and the Tidewater coasts of the South. Germans settled in eastern Pennsylvania. The French kept to the edges of the Atlantic, the Mississippi and the Saint Lawrence. The Spanish lived separately in the South and Southwest. People seemed to trade building ideas and develop new, mixed forms only in ethnically diverse regions like the Mississippi Delta, Quaker Pennsylvania, and the areas of New York and New Jersey colonized by the Dutch.

This isolation gave our first buildings styles that reflected their regional cultures. Old-world building customs were just adapted to the new climate and the new culture of making land. Cleared wood, field stone and mud bricks simply replaced plaster, quarried stone and thatch. Innovations were few and occurred only when forced by our cantankerous weather. Most American family farms held on to their regional forms and subsistence methods for two hundred years.

But in the 19th century, everything changed.

The years between 1815 and 1885, were America's most formative. That period saw the development of democracy, religious revivals, the end of slavery, the settlement of the West, the creation of countless new communities, dramatic improvements in transportation, industry and communication, and a huge increase in population fueled by immigration. In rural areas, where the majority of the population lived, the time marked an almost universal change from the old subsistence farm to a progressive, mixed economy of home produce, market farming and home industry. The farm country that we view today as peaceful and stable was in revolution, with new villages, new buildings, new farms and the complete renovation of old ones.

The West, starting in Kentucky and Ohio, was opened to homesteaders. Throughout the 1800s, the government made most of its revenue from land sales.

Emigrants from the old states and immigrants from the old world came for cheap, fertile new land. They hopscotched each other to claim their acres. For the first time, on a large scale and across a broad landscape, our cultures mixed. In the patchwork of parcels, a new American community grew. Neighbors had different languages, customs, clothes, foods and religions, but the same goals. They broke the same soil, battled the same plagues, weathered the same climate and shared the same crack-of-dawn to dark workday.

They also shared a remarkable enthusiasm for new ideas. They tested new crops and breeds. They traded recipes and seeds across fences. They exchanged the results of new experimental methods across the country, through books and farm journals. They started calling themselves progressive. Others called them book farmers. In the mid-19th century there were 59 different farm journals, many with larger circulations than urban magazines like *Harper's Monthly* and *Godey's Lady's Book*. "Taking a journal" meant subscribing to the best methods of farm management.

Farmers built fairgrounds, exhibition halls and corn palaces to meet with and learn from each other. They developed the Grange system for sharing storage and shipping expenses. They invented countless new tools. They searched the corners of their neighbors' barns and the corners of the world for new things to try. Each farmyard became a world atlas: Poland—

"Starting for the Fair," Drawn by W.M. Cary, *The American Agriculturist*, 1879

China and Yorkshire hogs; Peking, East India and Mandarin ducks; Spanish Merino sheep; Sebastapol and Toulouse geese; Belgian goats; Brahma, Sumatra and Guinea hens; Dutch Holstein cows; and Norman horses. Fields were seeded with Egyptian grass, Chinese sorghum, Guinea grass and Indian millet.

The farm families' table mapped their new taste for the exotic. New foods included Guinea squash (eggplant, from West Africa); Brussels sprouts, cardoon (a North African artichoke), Jerusalem artichoke (sunflower root—from South America), gumbo (okra—from Africa and a long time staple among southern African-Americans), Swiss chard, colewort (collard greens with an English-sounding name), and yams (a South American sweet potato cultivated by African-Americans because of its similarity to the true yam of West Africa).

The best evidence of the new spirit was how different regional vernacular building traditions were blended together in a new, mixed, American style. The sturdy, English medieval timber frame was retained for the skeleton of many houses and most barns. Following the Louisiana French, foundations were raised to allow dry houses and usable, well vented cellars. Foundation stone walls were chinked and mortared, like German barns, to keep out vermin and moisture.

Wraparound verandas, which had ancestors in India, Africa and tropical America, cooled and shaded living spaces and allowed rainy-day work areas. Closed wood stoves from Sweden and Holland eliminated the dangerous, drafty, inefficient open fire and freed the home interior of the mass of fireplace masonry. The German bake kitchen and Southern summer kitchen translated to a separate kitchen ell with an open porch where an iron cook stove would serve in hot weather.

The construction of an extra first floor bedroom mixed the traditional idea of a "birthing room," or nursery, with a practical response to the new emigrant and commercial cultures. Almost every farm was also an inn, and most rural travelers preferred the accommodations of a well kept home to those of dirty, crowded village taverns. Rooms were more spacious, and the food was better. Letting rooms was a source of revenue, entertainment and education. Conversations with travelers brought news and new ideas. Immigrants, staying each night at a different farm on their westward trek, would be acclimated to American methods and designs before they built their own farmstead. It also was common for farm sons to raft a year's harvest down the nearest tributary of the Mississippi to New Orleans, or through the new canals to Philadelphia or New York. The long walk back, with overnight visits to countless farms, was essential to the young farmers' education. An extra bedroom was rarely empty.

Big, three-bay, gable-entry New England barns were still the farmer's pride, but they changed too. They were already a mix of English and Dutch ideas, but now they were molded to invention. New open frames allowed hay forks to glide below their rafters. Stone cellars in the Pennsylvania German fashion provided winter-warm and summer-cool shelter for livestock. Chutes, pulley lifts and new machines eased work. Dutch doors, which originally kept animals out of houses, now kept them in barns. Big ventilators, like Italian cupolas, kept mildew from grain and gave a monumental appearance. Paint, usually white or red in the German tradition, preserved the boards. Big, bright barns could be seen as far as country church spires. They became signs of the new progressive farm where travelers, customers, and bartering neighbors could expect the best lodging, products and produce.

Other barn styles were experimented with too; farmers borrowed ideas from Canada to Louisiana and tried new sizes and new shapes. Small barns, in the old English side-entry style, became popular again. They were more easily cut into a hillside site. Barns banked into a hill or berm allowed an open-sided cellar, again in the German way. Small barns were the start of homesteads, field barns on big farms, or second barns for specialty stock. Built with tight, mortised and pegged frames, they were incredibly flexible. Farmers hitched yokes of oxen and dragged them to new locations as needed. A homesteader's first barn could become a carriage house or the structure of a bigger home as the family prospered.

The house and barns were complemented by an array of other structures; carriage houses, springhouses, woodsheds, outhouses and icehouses were common. Specialized buildings like dairy sheds, tanneries, cobble shops, stables and henhouses accommodated the farmer's industry. The whole farm was organized around a work yard that mimicked the classic courtyards of Rome and Greece. The concept of the rural courtyard arrived from Italy before most Italian immigrants. It was popularized by Thomas Jefferson and other Virginia planters from published plans by Andrea Palladio, a 16th century Venetian architect. The efficient procession of buildings also mirrored the production lines of Eastern mills and factories.

Country folk also developed a taste for style. They culled details from images in their magazines and journals; from architects' plan books; and from popular print publishers like Currier & Ives. They liked the classic revival styles and built columned entrances, models of Greek and Roman temples, to give their homes the same dignity that statehouses and courthouses had. They built wide roof overhangs, from the new Italian styles, to give shade and to protect walls from rain. They built Gothic gables for attic ventilation. Decorations were used if they were durable and simple to build. Decorative brackets were popular. Placed below roof overhangs, they were protected from the weather. Classic entry columns and fancy, turned porch posts were common. Again, they were protected by roofs. Doors and windows took on pretty shapes.

But the overriding design motif was progress. Everywhere the plan was prosperity; homes and barns were designed to grow. Old houses of frame, planks or logs became the kitchen ells of bigger homes. When they were wrapped in clapboard and pretty verandas, the hard times were hidden. Pioneers sawed flat faces on their logs and squared the corners of their huts in preparation for a finer future. Yards were arranged to allow for expansion. Everything was built on the square so that old walls would be plumb with the new. New doors and windows were little trouble cut from soft wood walls. Paint, adopted first just to preserve wood, became a tool for change. New buildings and old were swabbed in the same color to appeared as one and to show off the progress.

The new, proud, square-edged and freshly painted farmstead became the symbol of a mania that swept the countryside. "Good Order" was a catchall slogan for cleanliness, honest business dealings, abstinence and a neatly kept home. Its proponents pushed it with religious fervor. Books, prints and papers compared "Farmer Snug" and "Farmer Thrifty," who were tidy, trustworthy, progressive sorts, with "Farmer Slack" or "Squire Slipshod" who were slovenly drunks. The orderly appearance of a farm or shop was equated with the quality and purity of its produce. Nineteenth century Americans, who were not very tolerant of uncommon religious beliefs, accepted the Shakers, or at least their seeds and manufactured products, be-

Neglect and Poverty.

THE neglected home, where the
child grows up without knowledge
of order or correct system; tools and
vehicles exposed to all kinds of
weather, rusting and falling to pieces
from inattention.

Order and Thrift.

THE home of neighbor Thrifty, where
the children learn habits of neatness, economy and good management;
there being a place for every implement
when not in use, and each kept where
it belongs.

A progressive farmer pictured, book in hand, with a happy, healthy family, in a well furnished home.

"A Farmer at Home" from Sereno Edwards Todd's *Country Homes,* 1888

cause the Shaker creed included purity and honest dealings and because the structure of their communities epitomized good order. In 1868, an editor of the *American Agriculturist* thought that all the evils of farm trade would be solved "if everyone who sends things to market would be a 'Shaker.'" Business writer Thomas Hill saw the salvation of the nation's youth in a neat toolshed.

It's not a coincidence that Farmer Slack's place looked remarkably like the old subsistence homestead. Illustrations show free-ranging animals and old, regional-style buildings. Slack's place and the past were weathered wood. Order, abstinence, book learning, scientific management and fair dealing were the ways to prosper and the ways of the future. Prosperity went with a freshly painted white house, a neat yard and a big barn.

Old, regional farm structures, like this Hudson Valley Dutch barn and hay barrack, were equated with old-time methods and poor farming.

"The Shiftless Farmer" from Sereno Edwards Todd's *Country Homes,* 1888

A Villa in the Pointed Style, by A. J. Davis, Architect, from the 1842 book *Cottage Residences*, by A.J. Downing

Chapter 2

Building from Books

Plan Book Architects & Book Farmers

Sherry and Paul Durnan felt strange about their new old home. It's a 1890s carved gingerbread gem in Windham, New York farm country. They bought it on impulse after admiring it for years, but when they moved in, they started to get the sensation that they had been there before. The shape of the rooms, the layout, the sculpted woodwork, the staircase all seemed too familiar. Déjà vu usually flashes by in a moment. The Durnans lived with theirs for months. They both knew that they had been in the house before; they just couldn't remember when.

That Thanksgiving, while visiting Paul's brother and his family, part of the mystery was solved. Dick and Carlyne Durnan's home in Northport, on Long Island, was almost identical. It was that house that Sherry and Paul remembered. Except for a little difference in the gingerbread, the homes were the same. But why would two homes, built 150 miles apart be so much alike?

They are plan book houses. By amazing coincidence, both homes originated on page 74 of an 1894 plan book called *New Model Dwellings and How Best to Build Them* by Tennessee architect George F. Barber. A family on Long Island and farmers in upstate New York were both drawn by Barber's pretty perspective sketch, good country house plan and claim that the house "is handsome, massive and durable, and of such a character that it stands out bold and individualized among all others."

The Windham house was built as a retirement cottage in 1895, for farmers Phoebe and Silas Munson. They left the active work of the family farm to their children but continued to help by growing apples and cooking for summer boarders. Taking in summer vacationers from New York City had become a mainstay of the Munson farm, and perhaps the stylish new cottage was selected to appeal to the visitors' taste. It was like nothing else on the farm. The Van Siclen family

15

Sherry and Paul Durnan's house in Windham, New York, Barber's design number 61, and Carlyne and Dick Durnan's Northport, New York, home.

built the Long Island home in 1900 on a seven-acre country hillside. They loved the house but soon felt the location was too isolated. They moved into town and built another copy of the house. That's one advantage of a plan-book home.

When Barber taught himself how to draw, there were no standards for the title "architect." A century before, there were no architects in America at all. There was little to design in a building. Until the first decades of the 19th century, people just built whatever their neighbors did. Homes had characteristics that reflected their region and rarely presented a new style. Designs were based on old-world cultural traditions honed over the years by America's weather. New England farmers lived in New England farmhouses. Exiled Acadians in Louisiana built Cajun barns. German-Americans in Pennsylvania built stone homes just as their grandparents had. It was as simple as that.

The building process was fairly straightforward too. The property owner would contract a framer and discuss room size and layout. If external appearance was a concern, their conversation might turn to sim-

ilar homes built in the neighborhood. The framer was a skilled tradesman, with the tools and experience to turn trees into the tightly mortised posts, beams, sills and joists that formed the structure of most homes and barns. He would calculate a list of timber species and sizes that the owner would then provide. Most frames came from their site. The owner would cut trees to length and, if he was skilled or had access to a saw mill, might dress the timbers to size. He'd store them to dry, turning them so that they would keep straight. The framer would return to cut the joints and supervise a frame raising that would usually required a good-sized crew of the owner's neighbors and relatives. The owner would then cover the frame with wood clapboard or shingles and hire a mason for any stone or brick work. Fine woodwork like doors, windows and cabinets was contracted to another tradesman, a carpenter or joiner. The process was very much the same, throughout most of America, for our first two hundred years.

But our 19th century building boom attracted a new type of tradesman. Architects emigrated from Europe and plied their craft. Some Americans traveled to Europe for training. Others stayed and built and scribbled enough to call themselves architects. These new professional designers had to present some clear advantage over common builders and old-time methods, so they positioned themselves as artists and arbiters of fashion. They introduced the idea of applying an artificial style to buildings, an appearance not formed from tradition or environment. Through style they secured their income. Folks who wanted to be fashionable had to hire these artistic draftsmen for their latest whims. And, because what was in fashion could easily change, they had to hire them again and again. At a time when homes were simple to build, with little or no internal mechanical systems or sophisticated structural engineering, architects were essentially unnecessary. They responded to that fact by creating a new market for style.

Of course, that market was extremely limited. Very few Americans could afford fashion in their home designs. The first architects' clients tended to be wealthy suburbanites. They conducted their businesses or professions in or near the cities but lived in the nearby countryside. They commuted by the new railroads or steamships to avoid city squalor. They maintained, and were maintained by, servants. They were the "esquires" who thought of themselves as old-world squires on country manors. They named their homes after English country seats like "Blithefield," "Elm Grove," and "Raven Hill."

These faux feudal folk represented the smallest fraction of our society, so architects soon turned their attention to the building boom in the more rural countryside. Designer Andrew Jackson Downing knew that "for every twenty persons who live in villas, suburban cottages or town houses, there are eighty persons who live in farm houses." Immigrant architect Calvert Vaux "noticed the inexhaustible demand for rural residences." Downing saw "the evidences of growing wealth and prosperity of our citizens." But, to capture a share of this new market, they needed a new medium for their art. For their original clients, their services included face to face presentations, site inspections, and dickering with construction craftsmen. That type of work confined them to their own regions. They needed a way to sell their services to the immense audience of rural builders across the country. Their answer was the plan book.

Plan books were already popular in England. Downing started the American craze in 1842 by borrowing the format and style of J.C. Loudon's *Encyclopedia of Cottage, Farm and Villa Architecture and Furniture*, which was published in London nine years earlier. Downing's book, *Cottage Residences*, was a compilation of just ten home designs with landscaping advice and flowery philosophy. The designs and the prose were wonderfully ornate and the perspective illustrations, by architect Alexander Jackson Davis, were exquisite. The book was a great success and was followed in short order by similar tomes by more than a hundred different architects.

Downing's 1850 book, *The Architecture of Country Houses* sold over 16 thousand copies. Later books, which offered construction plans by mail, were more popular still. In 1887, Publisher Robert Shoppell claimed that over 12,000 American homes had been

Illustration from Frank J. Scott's *The Art of Beautifying Suburban Home Grounds*, 1872

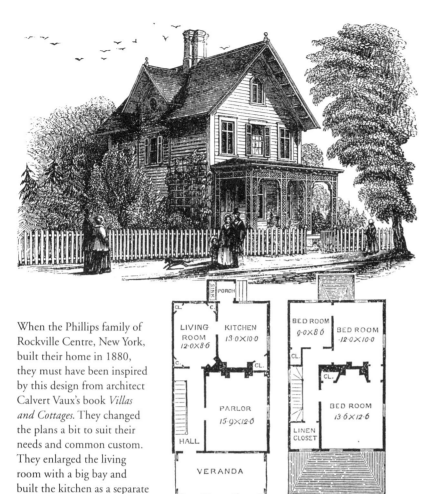

When the Phillips family of Rockville Centre, New York, built their home in 1880, they must have been inspired by this design from architect Calvert Vaux's book *Villas and Cottages*. They changed the plans a bit to suit their needs and common custom. They enlarged the living room with a big bay and built the kitchen as a separate ell at the back of the house.

PLAN OF PRINCIPAL FLOOR   PLAN OF CHAMBERS

built from his plans. In the 1890s, George Barber needed a staff of thirty draftsmen and twenty secretaries to keep up with orders for plans. His designs were built in every state.

The popularity of the early books is somewhat surprising. Late in the century, as homes became sophisticated with plumbing and heating systems and finer finishes, inexpensive construction drawings were a boon to builders. But the early books filled no real need. Building traditions were established and traditional builders were available in every community. Country folk already had a sense of style. The had a strong affinity for the classic buildings of Rome and Greece. In 1815, when the war-charred walls and columns of the Executive Mansion in Washington were triumphantly restored and painted white, the whole countryside was whitewashed in celebration. Classic details became symbolic of strength, dignity and success. White wooden "carpenter classic" homes were everywhere.

It seemed, at first, that the books succeeded because the architects had again created a new market. Just as they had before, they used the idea that architecture was art and fashion. They tried to convince their readers to abandon their traditions and their old dependence on the classic vernacular. Plan-book architect Gervase Wheeler told country builders that they could now build on a higher level. "The knowledge of the principals of design—the art of architecture" was available to all, now that he had published his book. Calvert Vaux let country folk know that they had been wasting their energy and their money on "meager, monotonous, unartistic buildings." Henry Hudson Holly added that "the planning of a country house is something so peculiar and intricate, and demands careful study of so many outlying considerations, that none but an architect can do it justice." After building on their own for all the preceding generations, country builders must have been startled by the news.

The architects too must have been startled as they sold their books and waited for their artistic homes to be built. It didn't happen.

It's a bit of a history mystery that the early plan books were so popular in the country, while the homes they presented weren't. Looking at the plans themselves, there is no mystery. The architects were city folk, and most just didn't understand country life.

Architects were successful with their wealthy suburban clients because they lived close to them, socialized with them and understood their needs. They never did the same with their country customers. While the vast majority of Americans were farmers, the vast majority of plan book homes were not suitable as farmhouses. Farmers wanted big kitchens that opened to their yards and to the street. They wanted verandas, efficient layouts, a farm business room, a small parlor and, always, a first floor bedroom. Architects only rarely provided a bedroom on the first floor; they often kept that floor exclusively for formal entertaining. They drew basement kitchens, servants' wings, drawing rooms and big halls for parties. Architects were still designing urban and suburban homes for the gentry.

In the plan books, when an architect's design was based on a previously built home, its owner was usually identified as a merchant, an attorney, a judge or a doctor. Homes designed for a specific tradesman or farmer were rare. Farmhouses and laborers' cottages were often identified as "models," which implied that they had never been built. Even these models betrayed the architects' focus. A.J. Downing's

Continued, page 22

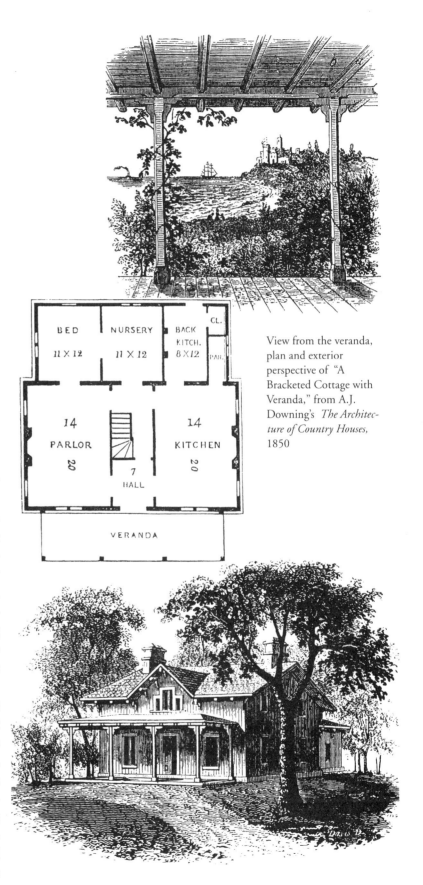

View from the veranda, plan and exterior perspective of "A Bracketed Cottage with Veranda," from A.J. Downing's *The Architecture of Country Houses,* 1850

A REMODELED FARMHOUSE

Henry Hudson Holly,
Country Seats,
1863

The architect, in the discharge of his duties, is called upon to perform many severe tasks, but none more arduous than that of remodelling a country house, where he has to contend with the blunders and conventional distortions of "carpenters' architecture," to develop harmony out of discord, beauty out of ugliness, elegance out of the commonplace. Consider, reader, how you would appall an artist of recognized ability by applying to him to finish a picture commenced by one who had no more exalted idea of art than what might be acquired in the aesthetic meditations of house and sign painting; how you would shock a Hosmer or Powers by presenting for the finishing touches of their delicate chisels some rude sculpture attempted by an ordinary stonecutter. Would not the enthusiastic devotee of art wonder at your applying to such a source at the first, and still more when you would have him remodel and give to the ill-used marble character and expression ? Would he not, with all the eloquence inspired by his profession, remonstrate against your course in employing at the outset so inferior an artist, and earnestly set forth the difficulty of overcoming the many radical errors of the inexperienced tyro? Would he not justly fear the injury he might do his own reputation by undertaking it at all . Yet every day do we see men of wealth, and sometimes of intelligence, applying to ignorant builders, self-styled architects, to furnish designs for cottages, villas, or even mansions of great pretension.

For in that very worthy class of mechanics, some one may be found in every town, whose ambition or conceit has so led him astray from his true path, that we find him rushing in where artists might fear to tread, and leaving such traces of his folly as render the whole neighborhood hideous with the whims of his untutored imagination. He may "draught a plan" which on paper will deceive the eye of the client, and actually persuade him into the delusion that, as it is the composition of a "practical man," it will appear well when erected. For many have thus unfortunately built in haste, and repented at leisure.

The usual resort in such cases, after the building is spoiled, is to apply to an architect of recognized ability to remodel the work. With perplexed brain the professional man sets about his expensive and difficult task of correcting that which, had it in the outset been properly done, would have saved both himself and the owner much vexation and annoyance.

Articles like this one, by New York City architect Henry Hudson Holly, show the attitudes shared by many of the professional designers who published plan books.

This design represents a cottage which the author remodelled for Dr. C. W. Ballard, at Noroton Darien, Connecticut. The original structure, which is shown in the vignette, was purchased by its present owner of a farmer, and is a good specimen of the small farm houses or cottages of Connecticut. Devoid of beauty, grace, or expression, pinched and contracted in all its features, placed usually in the most unattractive spot, directly on the road, with a formal avenue of cherry trees leading up to the door. These structures are indefinitely multiplied in the rural districts, and are the natural homes of a thrifty and enterprising, but unimaginative, tasteless, and perhaps overworked people.

The ceilings are low, and the rooms small, crooked, and without ventilation; green wooden shutters adorn the windows, and the outer walls, if painted at all, are sure to be of a staring white or a brilliant red; yet within the shadow of the humblest of these cottages have been born and reared some of the most distinguished men of our history. Perhaps there still exist, under such unpromising shelter, many "hands which the rod of empire might have swayed." Let it be our task to surround them with such refining influences as will render them better fitted for the higher and nobler life, and will smooth for them the upward path. Let us, in short, give them a home which may refine and elevate as well as shelter.

Yet, when a man of true taste and refinement comes in possession of so unpromising a subject as this, our drawing, we think, proves that with no considerable expense, effects of a striking and elegant nature may be produced, and the wholly unprepossessing building, under proper hands, be made comparatively a model of beauty no less than of convenience.

The vignette at left represents an ornamental well curb, and shows how that appendage, ordinarily so awkward and ungainly, may be made a pleasing feature of the grounds, and an earnest of the elegant hospitality of the residence to which it is attached. The well, ever grateful in its associations with memories of dripping coolness, in the parched summer time, of midday repose, and of many an office of friendship in the presenting of the cup of cold water to the weary traveller, should always be adorned with the most affectionate fancies at our command.

"Bracketed Cottage, with Veranda" is a simple design with a pretty good country plan, but the vista from the veranda shows a castle manor. Downing and the others seemed to always keep their old clients in view.

Much of what architects wrote about their new distant audience was less than flattering and betrayed their misunderstanding. Henry Hudson Holly called a client who hired him directly "a man of true taste and refinement," but, country carpenters, who he was selling his books to, were "ignorant mechanics" who "render the whole neighborhood hideous." Farmers were an "unimaginative, tasteless and perhaps overworked people." Other architects were a bit more tactful but held similar misconceptions. Gervase Wheeler ignored farmers, then more than eighty percent of our population, when he defined the three classes of people who built homes in the country as: commuters; retirees; and those who couldn't afford to live in the city.

And yet, country folk bought and read the books. Part of that is the simple fact that they were books; progressive, "book" farmers read everything from *Ivanhoe* to the *Journal of the London Zoological Society*. Their simple logic was explained in 1861, by an editor of *The Country Gentleman*, "The successful men in the business world are not those who merely labor hard with their hands, but those who think and plan much. Thought is developed by contact with other minds, either by talking or reading. Farmers, who have less opportunity than others for conversation, should supply the deficiency, as far as possible, by reading the thoughts of others."

They proved to themselves the logic of reading. Farmer Samuel Williams, of Waterloo, New York claimed, "I know a farmer who has paid over $300 for a private library and who takes both *The Albany Cultivator* and *Genesee Farmer*. In proof that he is something more than a theoretical farmer, he sold the surplus products of his farm last year for over $1400, and he paid out for the same but $90 for hired help— he has no children old enough to work in the field." In praising the editor of *The Cultivator*, Milton Ross of Allen County, Ohio, said it more succinctly, "Mr. Buel learned me how to raise one hundred bushels of potatoes from two bushels planting."

Editors of *The American Agriculturist* called the books they reviewed "brain manure" and said: "We have rarely seen a book written by anyone who felt that he had something to say...that did not contain some idea that was worth the cost of the book."

It's logical that some country readers got their money's worth just by skimming plan books for ideas. But, some actually became quite conversant with the styles, the terminology and the work of the different designers. Few New Yorkers today know that Calvert Vaux designed the buildings in Central Park. In 1865, farmers knew enough about Vaux to converse casually about his designs by their plan book number. Farmers seemed to know much more about the plan book architects than the other way around. They kept up constant correspondence, through their journals, about the merits of new plan books and the new building styles. That farmer who was "learned" by editor Buel would have seen architects' plans in reviews in *The Cultivator*. He would have known far more about home design than most architects cared to learn about potato farming.

Country editors usually kept their reviews in good order; they were polite and praised the best points of each new book, but hinted that improvements could be made. In 1845, on Downing's *Cottage Residences,* a reviewer in *The Cultivator* thought, "There are few, if any, plans into which changes may not be advantageously introduced." In 1858, on one of Gervase Wheeler's designs, the editor of *The Register of Rural Affairs* pointed out that "there is an unusually large provision for the entertainment of company, more than many will desire."

Farmers themselves were a bit more direct: "Try it again, Mr. Wheeler," said a correspondent to *The Horticulturist* in 1849.

A correspondent who called himself "Hawk Eye" from Keokuk, Iowa, wrote to *The Country Gentleman*, in 1855 that "Downing has given us a large number of beautiful exterior designs, and accompanied them with suggestions and remarks in such bewitching style as almost to defy criticism itself, yet to my eye when it comes to internal arrangements he signally fails— there is such an utter absence of convenience in a majority of the plans that any farmer's wife would be justifiable in holding fast to the old 'log cabin,' until better plans could be found." He added that architects failed because of "ignorance of the interior of the farmer's life."

Continued, page 24

PLAN OF A HOUSE.—Could not you or some of my brother subscribers, give me a design for a small house with four rooms—a drawing-room, dining-room, library, and bed-chamber. all on one floor, the house one story high.   I. E. O.   *Buckingham Co., Va.*

The accompanying plan will perhaps meet the wishes of our correspondent.   He says nothing of a kitch-

en—an indispensable apartment in every house.   Possibly he intends a basement kitchen; if so, the wing in the plan may be omitted—it saves, however, many steps and much fatigue, to place the kitchen on a level with the principal floor.

The plan needs little explanation.   The parlor and bed-chamber, (or nursery,) both open on the veranda, through a small entry for the exclusion of the direct cold air in winter.   If desired, another veranda may be placed in front of the hall, library and parlor, extending about two-thirds the length of the three, or the present one may be omitted.

The places for chimneys are not shown in the plan. Stoves or open fire-places may warm the nursery and parlor, by placing the chimney at the inner end of the closet between them; and the dining-room and library be similarly warmed by a chimney in the partition which separates them.

An improvement in the plan we have given, would be made by using the kitchen "closet" for a pantry, with a door opening from it directly into the dining-room; and using the "pantry" for a china-closet.

Engraving from R.K. Munkittrick's book *Farming*, 1891

Clippings from the New York farm journal *Country Gentleman* show how building ideas were shared and how they spread across the country.

In the February, 1856, issue, the editors filled a Virginia reader's request for a house plan. An Iowa reader responded to that layout in the May issue with the plan of the farmhouse he had built back in Ohio.

Countless other farmers would have clipped the plans or at least stored some memory of them for the time when they built on their own. You'll see echoes of these plans in other farmhouse designs in this book.

The requirements for a Virginia farmhouse, delineated by a New York agricultural writer, modified by ideas tested in the Midwest, became part of the common language of the American country home.

MESSRS. EDS.—In your paper of 28th February, seeing something said about plans of farm houses suitable for the mass of large farmers, I take the liberty of enclosing you a plan of a farm house built by me for my own use, which, for convenience and room, has been a good deal commended.   The house is 45 feet by 36, without wings, as I consider the nearer we can approach to a square form the more room we will get.

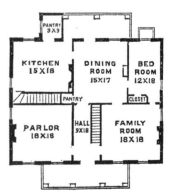

In this plan you will perceive that there is not an inch of lost space any where; every part is put to some good use.   There are 10 good rooms, (not one little one,) besides a large garret, and good halls above and below.

I built this house in Mahoning county, Ohio, three years ago, at an expense of about $1,800, the workmanship all being good, but plain.

I have given no plan for the elevation of the house, as it may be built after any of the modern forms.   WM. LITTLE.   *Muscatine, Iowa.*

Farmers wrote to architects, editors and reviewers to ask for practical plans and simple designs in what they called the American style, but soon recognized the need to learn, for themselves, how to plan their places on paper. One complained to *The Cultivator*, in 1845 that "those in the city, form their plans for city rather than the farm." Hawk Eye seems to have hit the mark when he said, "Farmers must learn to think for themselves—leave off undertaking to follow the fashions, customs and follies of the city or of their more wealthy neighbors, and make their houses as well as everything else bend to their own wants, necessities and tastes—learn to cultivate and exercise that independence which is by nature so preeminently theirs. In the next place they should make the subject of domestic architecture a study, and learn to make their own plans and designs."

They learned quickly and well. They designed buildings for themselves and even started publishing their plans, in direct competition with the architects. When farmer Lewis Allen published his own plan book, he introduced it by thanking his architect predecessors: "We owe them a debt of gratitude for what they have accomplished in introducing their designs to our notice," but continued, "They are insufficient for the purpose intended." Other farmers took an easier route, sending plans of proposed or recently completed buildings to their journals. Hundreds of their designs were published. They tended to be simpler than the architects' designs, and better in one important aspect: a larger proportion were not just design studies; they had been built and had proven themselves practical.

Plans of farm buildings in books and farm journals became a major form of communication between different regions. They tended to spread new design concepts and codify the best ideas. One example is the publication in an 1864 issue of *The American Agriculturist* of a Pennsylvania double-decked barn. The design was introduced in the spirit of the times: "The barns in different sections of the country vary in many points, and could plans of what in each section are considered models of excellence be presented, it would be very instructive."

Buildings and details of different styles and from different regions were mixed in what seems now like wonderful whimsy, but then usually had practical purposes. Gothic wall dormers let light and air into

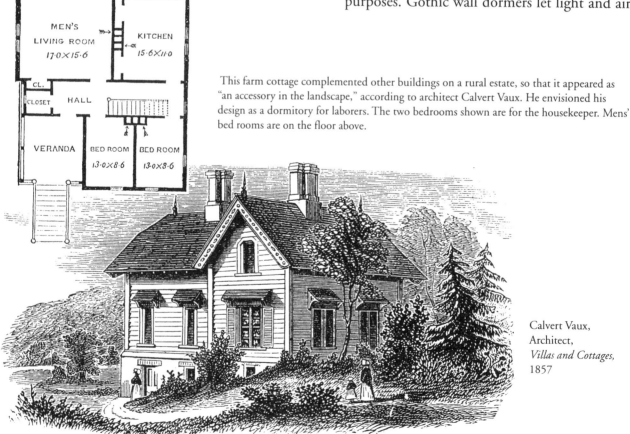

This farm cottage complemented other buildings on a rural estate, so that it appeared as "an accessory in the landscape," according to architect Calvert Vaux. He envisioned his design as a dormitory for laborers. The two bedrooms shown are for the housekeeper. Mens' bed rooms are on the floor above.

Calvert Vaux,
Architect,
Villas and Cottages,
1857

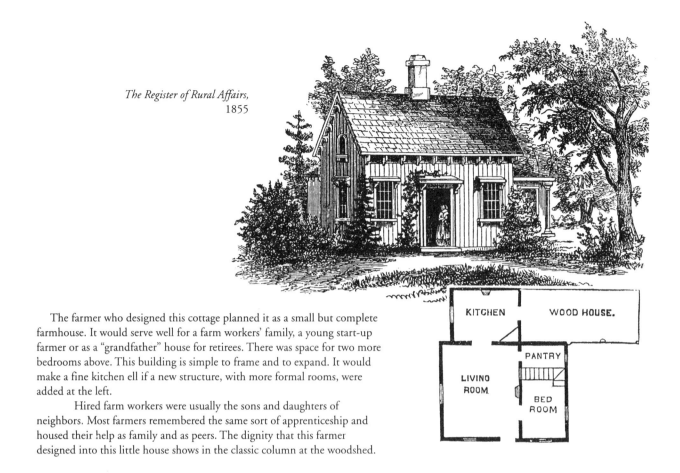

The Register of Rural Affairs,
1855

KITCHEN   WOOD HOUSE.

PANTRY

LIVING
ROOM

BED
ROOM

The farmer who designed this cottage planned it as a small but complete farmhouse. It would serve well for a farm workers' family, a young start-up farmer or as a "grandfather" house for retirees. There was space for two more bedrooms above. This building is simple to frame and to expand. It would make a fine kitchen ell if a new structure, with more formal rooms, were added at the left.

Hired farm workers were usually the sons and daughters of neighbors. Most farmers remembered the same sort of apprenticeship and housed their help as family and as peers. The dignity that this farmer designed into this little house shows in the classic column at the woodshed.

attics; deep roof overhangs of the Italian Villa and Greek Revival styles protected walls from wind blown rain, and Italian cupolas made great barn ventilators. Pennsylvania German stone cellars, ideal for sheltering animals and storing root crops, were dug under barns and houses from coast to coast.

Good designs were republished again and again. Lewis Allen's own barn, published in his book *Rural Architecture* in 1852, appeared at least a dozen times in farm journals and other plan books over the next 30 years. So, ideas and styles were mixed over long periods of time as well as over vast distances.

Architects should have been appalled by the new country buildings. They used a consistent style in each of their designs. Italian, Gothic, Tudor, and the old classical styles were never to be mixed on the same farmstead, let alone on the same structure. Downing had declared "unity" of style a strict rule. It was a high-style precept for a full generation of designers. Architects euphemistically called their most ornate designs "simple" if they displayed a single style in all the details. Yet, for some reason, they came around to the farmers' point of view. Perhaps it was the competi-

tion. Perhaps the farmers had, with their new graphic language, simply made their needs clear.

By the late 1860s, many architects' plan books included layouts that were similar to the farmers' own designs. Samuel Sloan's 1866, *Homestead Architecture,* had simple homes called "American," "Country," and "Plain" along with high-style villas. His earlier *Model Architect* had only the ornate. Architect Samuel Reed published good country plans each month in *The American Agriculturist* before compiling them into his books. David Hopkins, who went on to manage one of the largest plan catalog services, got his start entering farmhouse design contests in that same journal.

Architects even started mixing the styles in their designs. Their homes began to combine classic elements with their romantic ornaments, and common clapboard and shingles with their fancy masonry. They learned to appreciate the same design flexibility that farmer Lewis Allen celebrated when he said he was "free from the dogmas that are too apt to be inculcated in the professional schools." Architects simply called the free mix the Queen Anne style and declared it fashionable. Farmers must have been relieved.

AN ITALIAN COUNTRY HOUSE

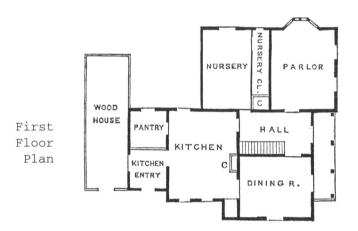

First
Floor
Plan

*The Register
of Rural Affairs,
1855*

The Italian style of building, characterized by its verandas, balconies, and projecting roofs, possesses several valuable qualities for country houses. It has more of an air of utility and adaptedness to the ordinary wants of American builders than the steep roofs and many angles of the Gothic style, while it has a freedom from stiffness and a grace of outline totally unlike the formal Grecian. The irregularity of form which it admits, enables the owner of an Italian dwelling at any time to add to it, if tastefully done, without at all injuring the architectural beauty of the whole. It is attended with none of the distortions of ceilings, so common in the steep-roofed Gothic, nor none of the uncomfortably heated apartments so often found connected with those in close proximity to a roof, unless

rafter ventilation has been carefully attended to.

We furnish above, an engraved view of a very convenient and moderate country house, possessing an Italian cast, perfectly simple in its structure, and entirely free from the campanile and other unnecessary decorations. The further roof seen in the view only covers, by its double sides, the parlor; while the nursery has a lower and separate roof, hipped like that of the veranda. The annexed plan sufficiently explains itself, c, c, being the places for the chimneys. In this plan, there are no receding angles, so subject to leakages when not made in the most careful manner. More architectural beauty, however would be imparted to the interior, if the roof over the parlor were made like that of the higher part of the building, or with a gable front.

Farmers borrowed high-style design elements for their homes only if they could fit their program of a good farm-house plan. They thought that the Italian style worked well because it was flexible and expandable.

The home in the farm journal engraving, at left, is aesthetically awkward but the plan is efficient. A. J. Downing's more elegant exterior, seen below, clads a layout that suited a lifestyle that was far too elegant for most Americans.

AN IRREGULAR VILLA IN THE ITALIAN STYLE

Andrew Jackson Downing, Architect, *Cottage Residences*, 1842

PRINCIPAL FLOOR

CHAMBER FLOOR

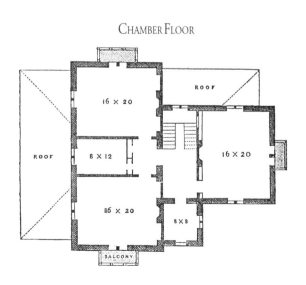

An Oriental Villa

Longwood, Natchez, Mississippi, Samuel Sloan, Architect.
Exterior View from *Sloan's Homestead Architecture,* 1866
Plan from *The Model Architect,* 1852

Throughout the 19th century, architects and farmers alike experimented with geometric shapes for their buildings. The octagon was first popularized by phrenologist Orson Squire Fowler in his 1848 book *A Home for All or, The Gravel Wall and Octagon Mode of Building*. Fowler's biggest contribution to building science was the "gravel wall," a reintroduction of the ancient technology of concrete. Today, he is remembered most for his odd-shaped houses.

Farmers liked the idea that the shape was economical to build and to heat. The designer of this little house felt that "the octagon form gives the greatest amount of interior space for given surface of outside wall." Architects liked the idea that their art was presented equally well from all views. Both soon learned that the shape sacrificed usable interior space and forced them into awkward rooms.

For homes, the square shape was generally adopted as the best combination of efficiency and useful interior space, while the traditional "L" was thought of as the most flexible house. L-shaped houses could be built in phases and were easy to expand. Octagonal and round barns, although not common, continued to be built. If stalls were arranged on the perimeter of those shapes, farmers could easily feed a big herd from a center manger.

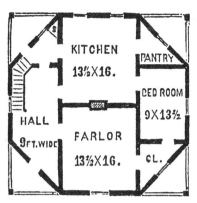

PRINCIPAL FLOOR PLAN

A SMALL
OCTAGON HOUSE

The Register of Rural Affairs, 1859

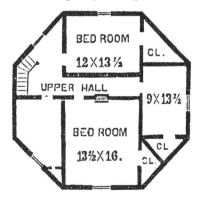

CHAMBER PLAN

English-born and trained architect Gervase Wheeler believed that Americans needed and wanted to be enlightened to the latest building fashions from Europe.

That wasn't the case. After this design was published in *The Horticulturist* magazine, letters from readers lambasted the plan. One corespondent asked, "Are we never to have any American cottages?" and continued, "Our climate is unlike European climates, particularly England; and why copy everything of the house kind, excepting in internal arrangements, from that country. But there are some things about this house, bating the gimp and pasteboard look of its outside, that I like; particularly its upper kitchen; and had it only that other indispensable appendage of a really comfortable house, a large family bedroom on the main floor, I should like the interior of it right well."

"Try it again, Mr. Wheeler; add on the bedroom; throw the roof into some sort of ship-shape; tack a light veranda on to the front as well, and then you will have quite a sensible house of it. What a wretched bother this filigree work makes when you want to want to repair a house."

An English Cottage

Gervase Wheeler, Architect, *The Horticulturist*, 1849

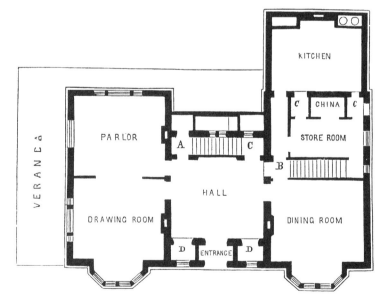

Principal Floor Plan

A SUMMER LODGE

Gervase Wheeler, Architect, *Rural Homes,* 1851

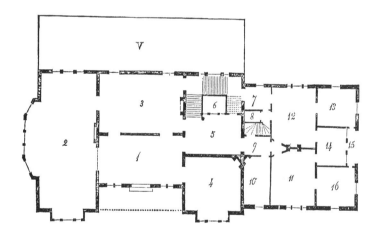

PRINCIPAL FLOOR PLAN

1, HALL; 2, DRAWING ROOM; 3, WAITER'S PANTRY; 4, LIBRARY; 5, INNER HALL; 6, CLOSET OR PANTRY; 7, COOK'S SERVING ROOM; 8, PLATE AND CHINA CLOSET; 9, VESTIBULE; 10, STORE ROOM; 11, SERVANT'S HALL; 12, KITCHEN; 13, SCULLERY; 14, LARDER; 15, BACK PORCH; 16, LAUNDRY.

Three years after his design for an "English Cottage," Mr. Wheeler did try again. In his book *Rural Homes* he presented a plan that was very similar, but which addressed some of the earlier criticism. The fancy trim work was gone and a simple veranda replaced the closed entrance porch.

Although the castle doors and lattice windows still hinted at Wheeler's English heritage. He claimed that his design was "suited to American country life" and at first glimpse that seemed right.

But the interior arrangement shows a house that just would not suit most Americans. The entire ground floor was given to formal spaces and servants' work areas. Most American country homes were designed around family kitchens and family living/dining rooms. Small, formal parlors were the norm but a Drawing Room, where a gentleman and his guests would draw away from household hubbub, was rare. Wheeler's idea that this was a "Summer Lodge" limited its appeal to the very small percentage of Americans who could afford two homes.

While Wheeler continued to misunderstand American country builders, the market for his book and his services must have been limited. Unlike other plan books of the day, *Rural Homes* was not widely reviewed, and the designs were not often copied in other publications.

The architect, like other unappreciated artists before and after him, was at least able to justify his own situation: "Unfortunately, however, there are very few who understand in what the excellencies of a house consist."

A House on a Farm

Gervase Wheeler, Architect, *Homes for the People*, 1855

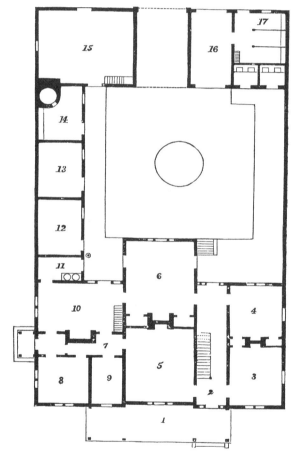

Plan of Principal Floor and Home Yard

1, Veranda; 2, Entrance Hall; 3, Private Parlor; 4, Sleeping Room; 5, Sitting Room; 6, Best Kitchen; 7, Hall; 8, Farm Business Office; 9, Storage Room; 10, Kitchen Work Room; 11, Wash Room; 12, Milk Room; 13, Fruit Room; 14, Feed House; 15, Wood House; 16, Wagon House; 17, Stable.

By the time Gervase Wheeler published his second book, *Homes for the People*, his ideas were changing. Like most emigrants, he was adjusting to the ways of his new country, and that showed in his work.

While the previous book argued that Americans needed manor houses, the new one focused on more practical concerns: the alteration of old buildings; how to lay out a farmyard; and how to mix paint.

As before, the new book included elaborately styled villas, but it also presented simple homes for "the respectable mechanic, or young beginner in business." One chapter addressed the special needs of American farmers. Wheeler's comments on farm houses were eloquent echoes of the criticism of his first design: "The farmer should leave to the proper proportions and outlines of his buildings, the chance of producing a pleasing effect...he needs no inch board finery and may trust the building to tell its own tale."

Wheeler's design for "A House on a Farm" has, as its core, the same H-shaped plan as his earlier designs. Its clipped gable ends and bark-covered porch posts are standards of English rustic cottage architecture. But the rooms are all American.

The Best Kitchen and Sitting Room are the family dining and living areas. They adjoin the Work Kitchen which is now the hub of the house. The Parlor, the only formal room, is small. There is a first floor Sleeping Room, the essential, flexible space that farmers used when needed as a nursery, sick room, apartment for elderly relatives, or bedroom for borders.

This plan is telling its own tale. It's the American house that Wheeler was asked for years before.

A cottage design by architect
George E. Woodward,
from the book
*Woodward's
National Architect,*
1868

Chapter 3

Villas
&
Cottages

Architects' Plans for the Country

The designs on the following pages are not at all typ-ical. These homes are here because their plans reflect the layouts that country families were looking for. They all have more area for family use than for entertaining and big, first floor kitchens. Most have a first floor bedroom, the kitchen in a separate ell and front and kitchen verandas.

These homes were not very popular with their de-signers. Most designs in 19th century architects' plan books had more rooms for formal entertaining and accommodations for servants. Many had basement kitchens. Most were also much more elaborate and elegant in their exterior design. They usually expressed the best points of each of a variety of the formalized styles. Gothic, Tudor, Norman and Italian designs were favored by architects. The last was also called Bracket-ed, for the ornamental supports of its widespreading roofs. Like artists who could work in different genres, who could paint portraits or landscapes, architects were usually adept in each of these styles.

They were not quite as artistic with these country plans. With some, they just cloaked them in high-

style ornament. That gave the same tacked-on look that architects derided when country carpenters did it. With others they seemed to try to work with the plainness as if it was another motif. They never em-braced a single style for these homes and never seemed to know exactly what to call them. A high-style home called "Gothic" would have pointy window shapes, steep roofs, vertical siding and fine-cut filigree. There was no word used constantly to describe these homes and no consistency in the image. Architects fumbled with their titles for these plans as much as they fum-bled with the look of their exteriors.

Part of the problem was a basic misunderstanding of the concept of a country family's home. Architects and their primary clients made their living in the city. They used and viewed country houses as places of rest and retreat. Their villas were the estate houses of gen-tleman farmers, retired from a profession or industry. Their cottages were smaller-scale retirement homes or vacation places. Like the seaside cottage in this chap-ter, they used their country places as temporary havens from the grime, crime and epidemics that plagued 19th century cities. If they lived full-time in the country they lived at a railroad stop or a steamboat dock, in villages linked directly to their places of income.

Real country folk usually worked right at home. They were farmers, blacksmiths, ministers, coopers and village merchants. Others, like country doctors, carpenters and peddlers were itinerants with their home at the hub of their travels. There was no haven from their travails. Their houses had to be efficient and flexible enough to be an office, a manufactory, a hospice, a hospital and a home.

The designs in this chapter are all from fairly late in the plan book era. Earlier books had few

Illustration from *The Rural New Yorker*, c 1870

plans, if any, that someone who lived in the country could live with. What made the architects change their ideas? In the next chapter, you'll see country builders' own designs for their homes. Those were drawn and published concurrently with the big city books. Just as country folk culled ideas from architects' designs, the architects seem to have borrowed back. Farmers' written suggestions weren't enough; the cultural gap was too wide and their words were misunderstood. When farmers and country builders started drawing plans, they started speaking in a language that urban designers could understand.

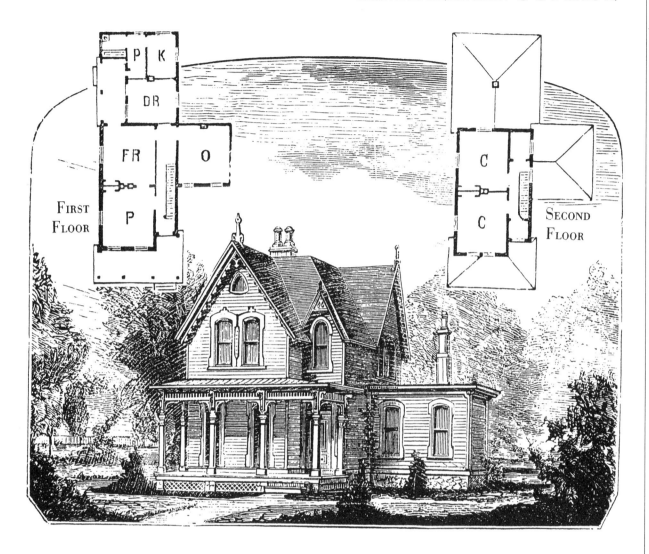

This design was drawn by us for the Rev. John D. McClintock, Huntingdon, West Va. It is one of those American cottages containing very liberal accommodations for a small family. Its cost, finely finished, of bricks, painted neat, with porches and well finished interior, was $3446.25; built of frame, would cost $3000. It is slated with slates from the True Blue Quarry, Pennsylvania. These slates come very regular in color, are durable and strong; ornamentally laid, they cost 12 cents per square foot. The hall and parlor are finished in chestnut and other natural woods, oiled and rubbed down. Care has been taken with the proportions. The windows are large, and the interior is finished with heaters, slate mantels, and range complete for this sum. Such buildings are needed, and we design numbers of them for various persons all over the country. They sell at good price and give universal satisfaction. Every situation demands different treatment, and the arrangements of the rooms can be suited to any locality and the taste of the owner.

First Floor: P, parlor, 15 by 16 feet; F R, family room, 15 by 16 feet; O, office, 15 by 16 feet; D R, dining-room, 12 by 14 feet; K, kitchen, 10 by 11 feet; B R, bath room, 6 by 7 feet; P, pantry; H, hall, 6 feet. Second Floor: C, chamber, 15 by 16 feet; C, chamber, 15 by 16 feet. —Issac H. Hobbs and Son, Architects, *Hobbs Architecture*, 1873

A Village Cottage

A.J.Bicknell, Architect, *Specimen Book of One Hundred Architectural Designs*, 1878
Plans: *Bicknell's Village Builder and Supplement*, 1871

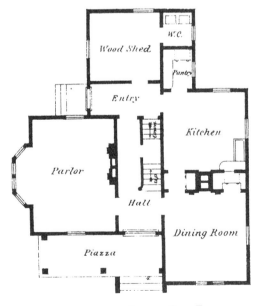

PLAN OF FIRST FLOOR

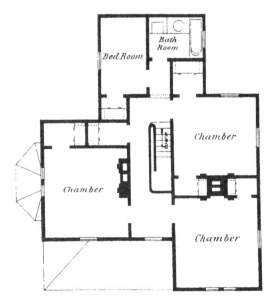

PLAN OF SECOND FLOOR

An Old-Fashioned Country House

George E. Woodward, Architect,
*Woodward's Cottages and
Farm Houses*, 1867

The design for this house was prepared to answer a popular demand, that shall embrace, at a low price, the long-prized excellencies of the old-fashioned country house, with hall through the centre and doors at both ends to give ample ventilation in warm weather. With all the progress that has been made in architectural convenience and embellishments, we doubt if the central hall and independent communication with all rooms have been much improved on. The finest country houses with which our associations are connected, and which are remembered for their comfort and elegance, had the spacious hall running through the centre.

It will be observed in this design, that as far as possible all angles have been avoided, and the construction planned for straightforward square work. The roof of the addition is nearly flat and tinned, and the ridge finished below the plate of the main roof. The principal roof is covered with slate, cut to a hexagonal pattern, has a square pitch, and except the connection with central gablet, is without valleys; the rooms are pleasantly located, easily reached, and for economy are as compact as any plan that may be devised of similar area. The exterior is plain, but, at the same time, it looks well, and will wear well, and while without the irregularities that afford variety of light and shade, it is also without the expense connected with them.

FIRST FLOOR PLAN

KITCHEN
16 X 13.6

6' X 3' CLOSET

PARLOR
23.6 X 14

DINING ROOM
16 X 14

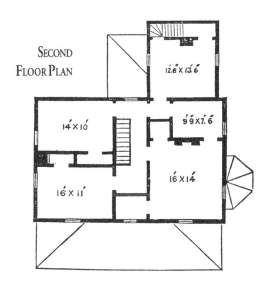

SECOND
FLOOR PLAN

12.6 X 13.6

14 X 10

9.9 X 7.6

16 X 11

16 X 14

A Farm House

The proportions of this house are good, and the form pleasing without being complicated; the impression produced on the observer by its general aspect is, that room, comfort, and convenience are within its walls, and that the dignity and hospitality of the gentleman farmer are manifested silently yet plainly by its external expression. It seems, however, in its architectural details to have borrowed somewhat from its city neighbor. We readily suspect that its owner has spent a portion of his life at something else than tilling the soil; that he has been a merchant or a physician, for we often hear of such changes of avocation in this country: at any rate, we must conclude that he is a farmer with some means, and a taste somewhat refined and cultivated by the company he has kept. Yet design looks essentially like a country house. It could scarcely be recognized as anything else; the few ornaments that it wears cannot disguise its native plainness; it has been born and bred in the country, and all the city polish that it has received cannot conceal the palpable fact. This design might be built in any part of the Union, without reference to the use implied by the appellation of "farmhouse" which we have here given it, and it would always be ranked as a country house of considerable importance.

Accommodation—The ample veranda in front, with its central feature, is worthy of notice; it seems to invite the passerby to walk in and share the repose and comfort that exist within. From this veranda we enter the hall F, 8 by 33 feet, which contains the principal staircase, and affords communication with all the best rooms on this floor. A is the parlor, 33 by 16 feet, entered by folding doors, and a good example of a regular, well-proportioned room; when we say well-proportioned, we mean according to our ideas of interiors, rather than in conformity with the rules based on classical authority for the regulation of internal proportions. Of course much depends on the height of the story; in this case it is twelve feet. B, 14 by 16 feet, is a library or sitting-room, or both, as the requirements of the family may dictate. The chief attraction of this room is the octagonal bay, a very pleasant feature, whether contemplated from within or without. The dining-room D is 16 by 18 feet, and on occasions of unusual festivity can be extended by throwing open the sliding doors into the room B. A nice closet to the dining-room is seen at I, and another for the occasional stowing away of various articles of use or wear, such as will readily occur to the mind of any liver in the country. G is a passage from dining-room to kitchen; and H a pantry, represented as shelved on both sides; from the passage G the private stairs extend to the second floor of the back building, which is on a level with the half-pace of the main stairs. The apartment E is designed for a kitchen, and by its dimensions, 15 by 22 feet, it may be readily inferred that we have a partiality for those good, old-fashioned country kitchens that our ancestors delighted in. Beyond this is a one-story apartment N, 12 by 15 intended for a multitude of uses which will not fail to suggest themselves to those acquainted with the requirement of farm life.

L, M and O, shown on the Principal Floor Plan are verandas. All of the rooms on the second level are Chambers, or bedrooms. The separate suite of rooms above the kitchen is for farm help. Sloan noted the common custom of laborers "not only lodging under the same roof with the farmer, but living on such terms with him that a stranger might with difficulty recognize the superior."

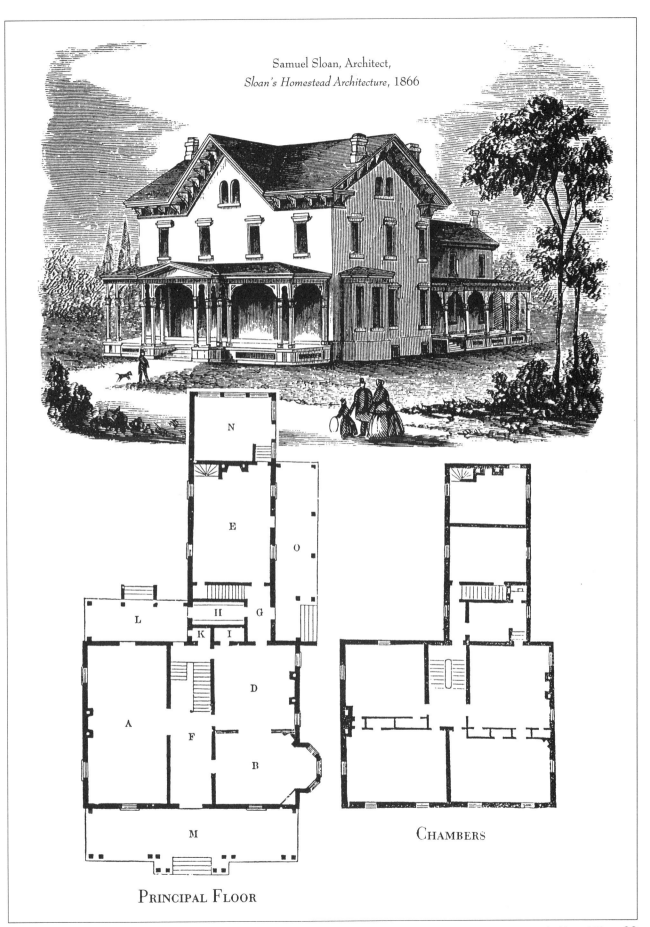

Samuel Sloan, Architect,
Sloan's Homestead Architecture, 1866

PRINCIPAL FLOOR

CHAMBERS

An American Cottage

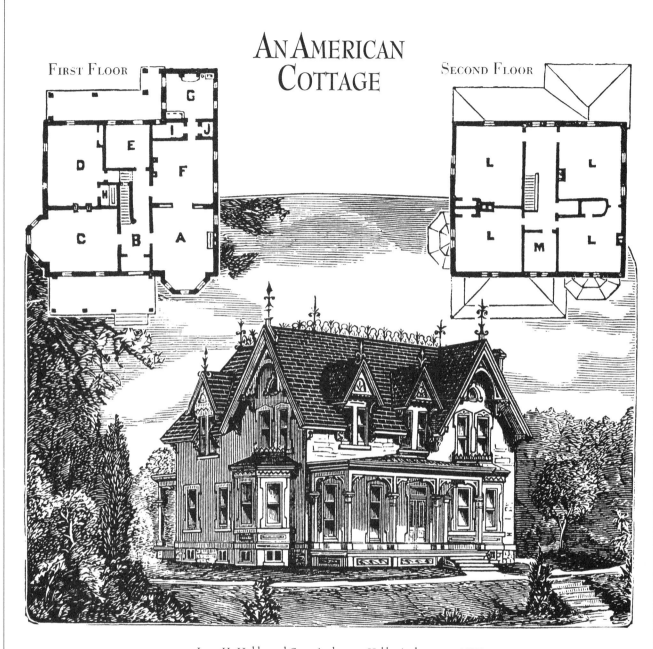

Issac H. Hobbs and Son, Architects,*Hobbs Architecture*, 1873

This design was organized for Mrs. Stabler, of Lynchburg, Virginia. It contains many desirable points, architecturally, and when constructed will be a bright and beautiful home, containing internally all modern improvements. It is designed to be built of bricks with hollow walls. The building will cost, when finished, between $5000 and $6000.

First Floor: A, parlor, 18 by 18 feet; B, hall; C, chamber, 18 by 20 feet; D, dining-room, 18 by 18 feet; E, smoking-room, 13 by 13 feet; F, nursery, 16 feet 6 inches by 23 feet; G, kitchen, 14 feet 6 inches by 14 feet; H, bath-room, 6 by 6 feet; I, storeroom, 10 feet by 4 feet 3 inches; J, china-closet, 4 feet by 4 feet 3 inches. Second Floor: L, chambers; M, sewing-room.

AN AMERICAN COTTAGE

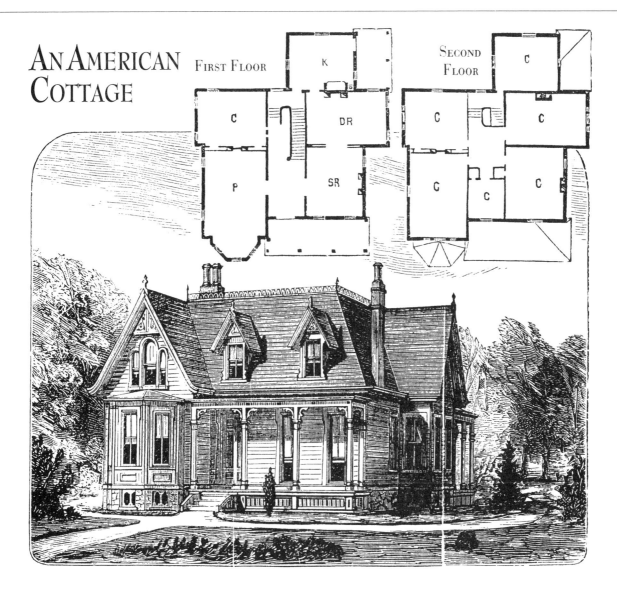

This design is a beautiful type of an American home. We have many orders for drawings of such styles of houses. Some people persist in filling their houses with closets, and, when in excess, they become hiding-places. There should be a commodious closet and clothes-press in every chamber. The kitchen should have ample places for its necessary articles; the store-room, butler's pantry, are all needed. This building can be built for $2500 very complete, by good superintendence on the part of the owner in purchasing materials, and seeing that they are used economically. The house is of frame, covered with felt and weather-boarding; this felt is now manufactured quite thick, and nailed upon the studding. The roof may be shingles or slate; there is an air space or loft above the second floor. An open communication from below the cornice must be made to communicate with it all around, and there must be two flues, one open at the bottom of this loft, and passing through the roof, and the other open at the top of loft, and opening out high above. This insures a constant change of air in the vault, and renders the upper rooms cool and comfortable at all times.

First Floor: H, hall, 10 feet wide; P, parlor, 16 by 22 feet; S R, sitting-room, 16 by 18 feet; D R, dining-room, 14 by 22 feet; C, chamber, 14 by 18 feet; K, kitchen 14 by 18 feet.   Second Floor: C, chamber, 16 by 22 feet; C, chamber, 10 by 10 feet; C, chamber, 16 by 18 feet; C, chamber, 14 by 18 feet; C, chamber, 14 by 22 feet, C, chamber, 14 by 18 feet. — Issac H. Hobbs and Son, Architects, *Hobbs Architecture*, 1873

A Farmhouse

These plans were designed for a convenient and comfortable Farmhouse in the American style, comprehending the most economical and practical methods of construction. The size and shape of such houses should be made to conform to the requirements of those who are to occupy them. Unlike the villager, the farmer has ample road front, and his house should be so arranged as to secure the most pleasant outlook from the living rooms.

Farm houses usually stand disconnected and apart from other buildings, and should have outlines that will best adapt them to the conditions that are otherwise manifest in the location. This plan is intended for an eastern frontage, where it would face the morning sun, when the principal and broader portions of the building, at the right, would be doubly valuable as a shield to ward off the northern winds from the parts of the house most used by the occupants. (By reversing the plan it would be equally adapted to the opposite, or easterly side of a road.)

It is intended that the body of the house shall be set at least two feet above the ground; this gives opportunity for good-sized cellar windows, that will admit light, and afford good openings for cellar ventilation, and also secure the frame-work of the building against moisture from the ground. Such moisture, if allowed, will cause decay of the sills and other principal timbers, and is sure to percolate upward into the house, filling it with unwholesome vapors.

The variety of the general outlines as shown in the elevation are calculated to impart a cheerful and lively appearance always desirable in a country home, and very pleasant to the passerby. The ridged roofs, with their spreading gables and ample projections, are features of frankness in which there is no attempt at concealment or imitation. The bay-windows, wide entrance, and spacious piazza, are each expressive of liberality and refinement. The extreme simplicity of the details, and methods of construction, devoid of all ostentatious display, clearly express the purpose of the building, and commend it to the consideration of all who are interested in rural house building.

Should it be desirable, the central portion of this house could be built first, and would be found quite sufficient as the dwelling house of a small family, and the remainder added afterwards as required.

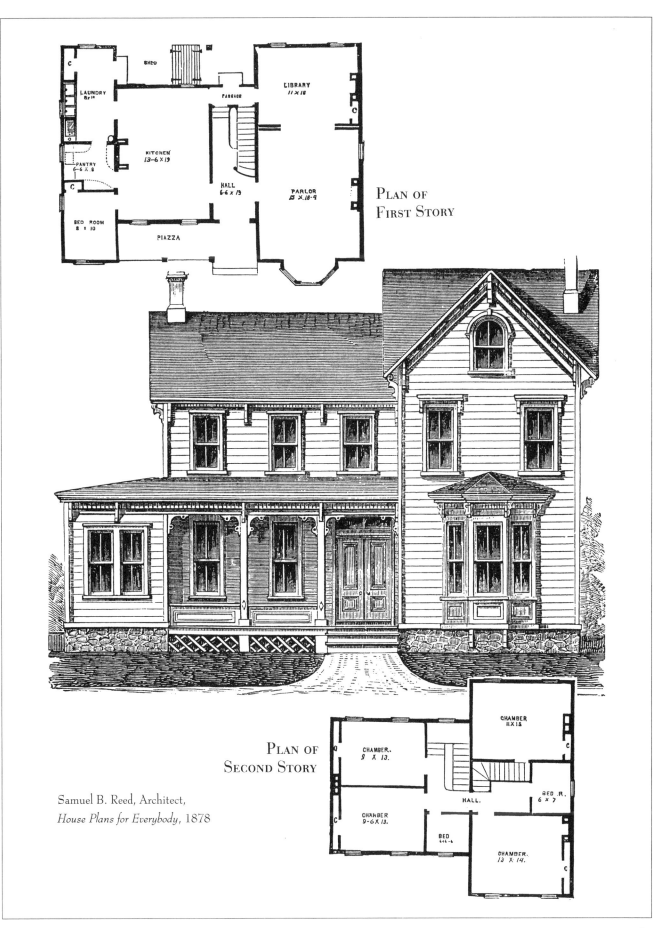

PLAN OF
FIRST STORY

LAUNDRY
8 x 10

SHED

PASSAGE

LIBRARY
11 x 18

C

PANTRY
6-6 x 8

KITCHEN
13-6 x 19

C

HALL
6-6 x 19

PARLOR
15 x 18-9

BED ROOM
8 x 10

PIAZZA

PLAN OF
SECOND STORY

CHAMBER
11 x 13

CHAMBER.
9 x 13.

C

CHAMBER
9-6 x 13.

BED
4-6-6

HALL.

BED.R.
6 x 7

CHAMBER.
13 x 14.

C

Samuel B. Reed, Architect,
House Plans for Everybody, 1878

A Cottage

Roussiter and Wright, Architects,
in A.W. Brunner's *Cottages, or Hints
on Economical Building*, 1884

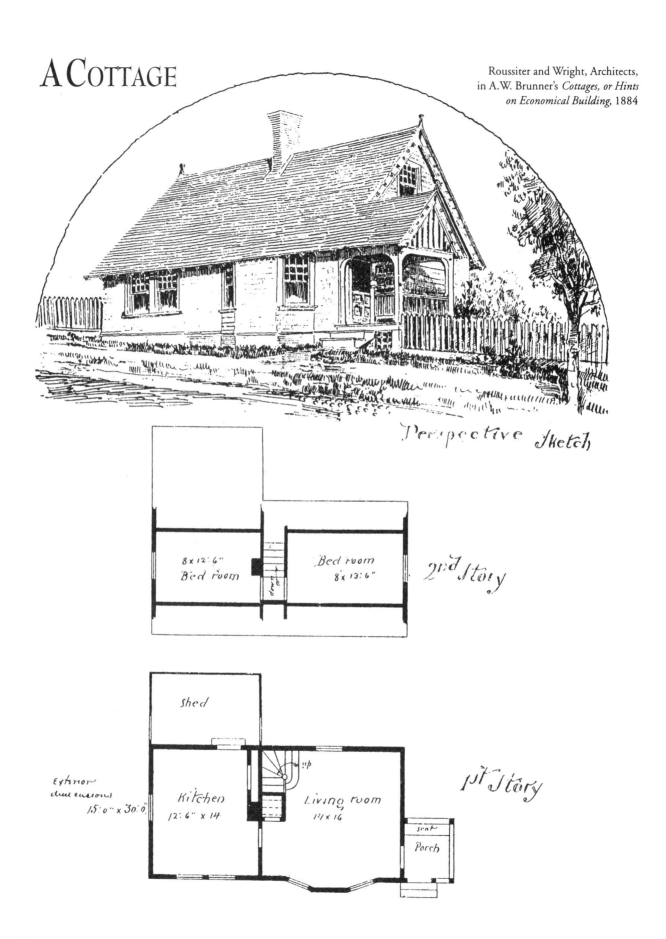

Perspective Sketch

2nd Story

8 x 12'6"
Bed room

Bed room
8 x 13'6"

1st Story

Shed

exterior
dimensions
15'0" x 30'0"

Kitchen
12'6" x 14

up

Living room
14 x 16

seat

Porch

perspective Sketch

A Seaside Cottage

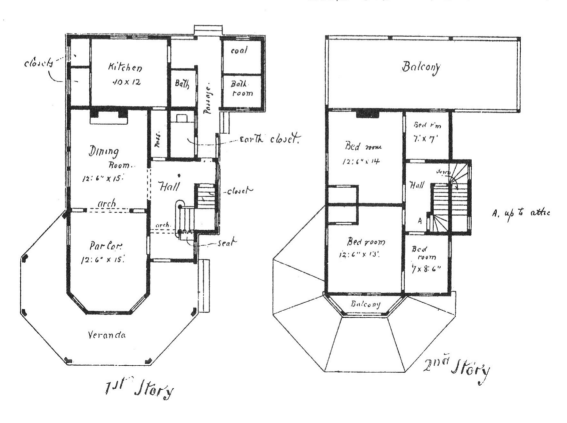

closets

Kitchen
10 x 12

coal

Bath

Bath room

Passage

Dining Room
12:6" x 15:

Hall

earth closet.

closet

arch

arch

seat

Parlor
12:6" x 15:

Veranda

1st Story

Balcony

Bed r'm
7: x 7:

Bed room
12:6" x 14:

Hall

A. up to attic

A

Bed room
12:6" x 13:

Bed room
7 x 8:6"

Balcony

2nd Story

Roussiter and Wright, Architects, in A.W. Brunner's *Cottages, or Hints on Economical Building*, 1884

A COTTAGE IN THE POINTED STYLE

This cottage was designed for a gentleman in Salem, Illinois. The superstructure is of brick, and the roof of slate, cut in ornamental shapes. It contains ample accommodations for a small family, and possesses conveniences, such as bath room, water closet, low-down grates, etc. The exterior is very pleasing, and is capable of a much higher degree of ornamentation than is shown in the engraving. The house can be built for $5000. It can be modified to preserve the external appearance; yet, by leaving out such conveniences as bath room, etc., which can be added to the house at any time in the future, it can lie built for $3000, if built of frame.

First Floor: A, hall; B, sitting-room, 16 by 16 feet; C, parlor, 16 by 20 feet; D, dining-room, 13 feet 11 inches by 20 feet; E, kitchen, 13 feet 11 inches by 12 feet; F, scullery, 8 feet 5 inches by 6 feet 4 inches; G, china-closet; H, sewing-room, 10 by 6 feet 4 inches.

Second Floor. I, bath room, 5 feet 2 inches by 8 feet; J, bedroom, 8 feet 6 inches by 10 feet; K, chamber, 13 feet 4 inches by 15 feet 2 inches; L, chamber, 13 feet 4 inches by 12 feet; M, chamber, 13 feet 8 inches by 15 feet 11 inches; N, chamber, 18 feet 9 inches by 15 feet; O, hall; P, balcony.

Issac H. Hobbs and Son, Architects,
Hobbs Architecture, 1873

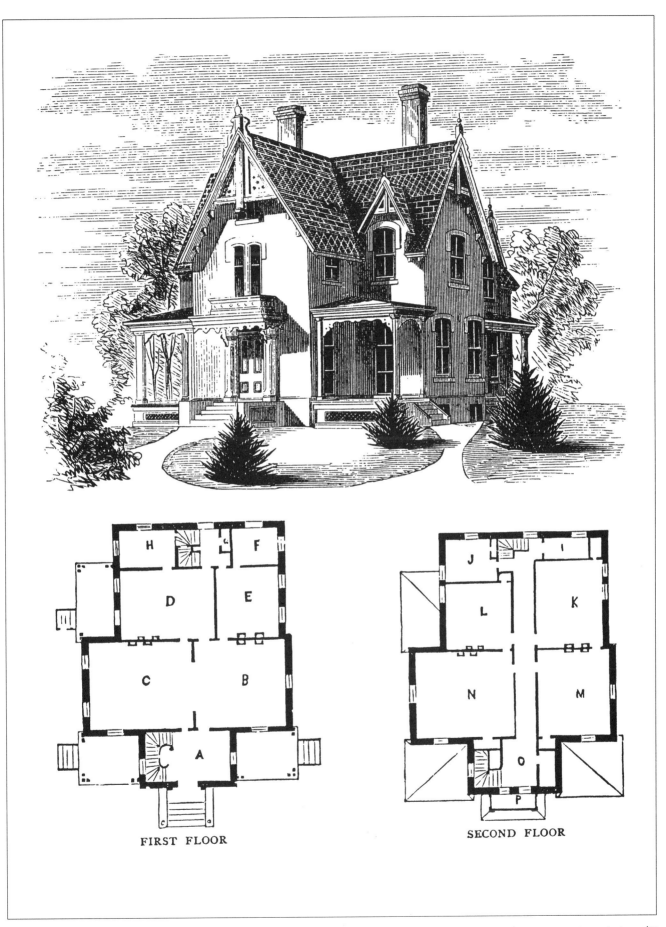

FIRST FLOOR

SECOND FLOOR

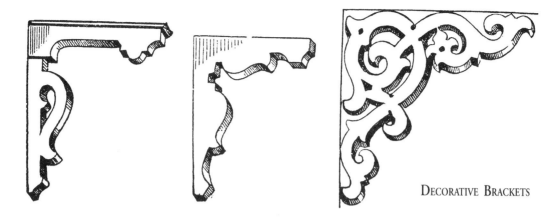

DECORATIVE BRACKETS

A BRACKETED AMERICAN COTTAGE

Samuel Sloan, Architect, *Sloan's Homestead Architecture*, 1866

We mean what we say when we pay this design the high compliment of calling it American, and we think our readers will sustain us in the application of the very comprehensive term. Simple in form, convenient and economical in arrangement, tasteful yet unassuming in detail, we know of no title so expressive of its deserts as the one we have given it. Although it possesses no trait preventive of its recognition as an important country residence in any part of the Union, we conceive that it would be a decidedly acceptable dwelling to the well-to-do resident of the Western prairie. The umbrage afforded the windows by the canopies and balconies, while enhancing the boldness of the design, contributes greatly to the comfort of the apartments by protecting the glass from the noonday summer sun, even in the Northern and Western States. On the other hand, the disposition of the fire-places is such as is best calculated to insure good draught in chimneys, and the retention of a greater proportion of the heat generated within the building.

Accommodations—From the front piazza F, the passage of 6 feet wide is entered, which gives access to all the rooms; an outside entrance is also given in the end of the building through the stair hall. A, 16 by 20 feet, is designed for a parlor; B, 16 by 16 feet, is a sitting-room; C, 16 by 20 feet, a dining-room; D, 16 by 16 feet, a kitchen; and E, a pantry, affording also a passage from dining room to kitchen. We may remark here, that a veranda extending the full length of parlor and dining-room would be a very beneficial addition to this design, both for use and appearance. In accordance with the apparent demand for such an improvement, we have shown it in the perspective. The divisions of the chamber plan are similar to those on the first floor, with the addition of closets on each side of the chimney fronts in all the chambers, H,— I being a wardrobe.

Construction—The great abundance of wood in some portions of our country, the facility with which it is transported from a timber region to a prairie, and the ease with which it is adapted to building, will be reason enough for using it for that purpose for generations to come. The design before us is intended to be constructed of wood.

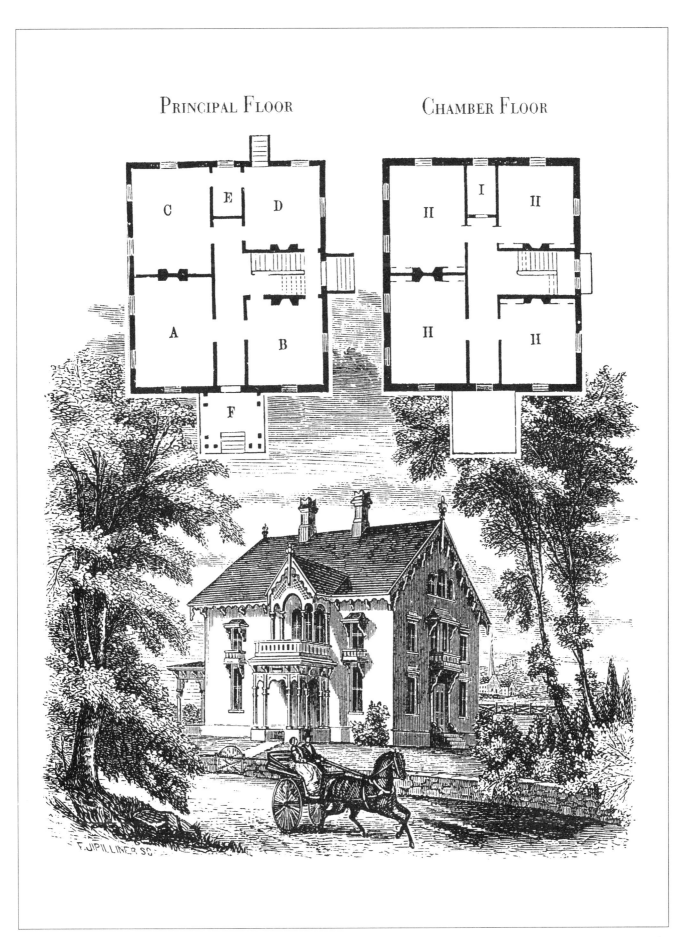

Principal Floor

Chamber Floor

C   E   D

A   B

F

II   I   II

II   II

F. JUPILLINER SC.

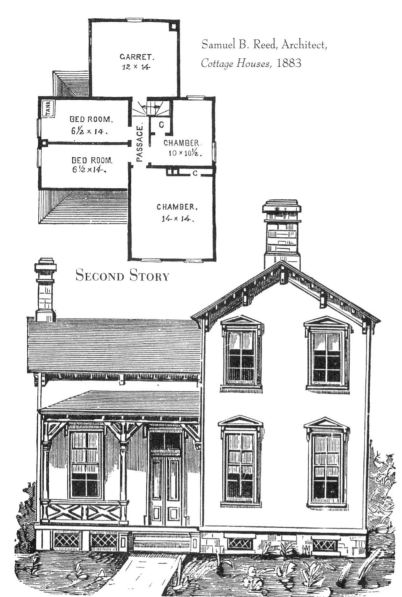

GARRET.
12 × 14

Samuel B. Reed, Architect,
Cottage Houses, 1883

TANK

BED ROOM.
6½ × 14.

BED ROOM.
6½ × 14.

PASSAGE.

C

CHAMBER.
10 × 10½.

C

CHAMBER.
14 × 14.

SECOND STORY

George E. Woodward, Architect,
Woodward's Cottages and Farmhouses,
1867

A WISCONSIN FARMHOUSE

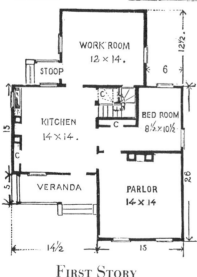

WORK ROOM
12 × 14.

12½

STOOP

6

C

KITCHEN
14 × 14.

C

BED ROOM
8½ × 10½

15

C

26

VERANDA

5

PARLOR
14 × 14

14½

15

FIRST STORY

These plans are partially based upon a sketch of a Wisconsin farmhouse. It is suitable to most places in this latitude, and may properly front towards any desired direction. The interior is adapted to the wants of an average sized family. As is usual in this class of buildings, all halls, and expensive stairways are omitted, the entire space being devoted to the uses and convenience of the family. The general outlines and style are such as predominate on the buildings of thrifty farmers everywhere, and are suggestive of comfort and modest pretentions. The woodwork is set 2 feet above the grading, giving room for cellar windows and insuring dryness of the interior. A veranda is always pleasant and useful to protect the front entrance from sun and rain.

This design was erected from our drawing, by William P. Debott, Union county, Indiana. It has a sandstone base, with window sills and heads of the same material. The superstructure is of bricks, shingle roof, covered with fire-proof paint, and its cost when fully finished was about $8000. We are constantly making for parties designs similar to the above, with varied evolutions, interior and external, in various parts of the United States, no two of which are ever precisely alike. Persons ordering such houses should be very careful to have every part, fully understood before commencing, and any thing short of full drawings will be found dangerous and expensive.

An American Residence

First Floor: P, parlor, 16 by 23 feet; S R, sitting room, 15 by 16 feet; L, library, 14 by 14 feet; D R, dining-room, 15 by 19 feet; C, chamber, 12 by 14 feet; K, kitchen, 14 by 16 feet; S, scullery, 11 by 14 feet. Second Floor: P C, principal chamber, 16 by 23 feet; C, chamber over sitting room, 15 by 16 feet; C, chamber over dining-room, 15 by 19 feet; C, chamber over library, 14 by 14 feet; C, chamber over chamber, 12 by 14 feet.

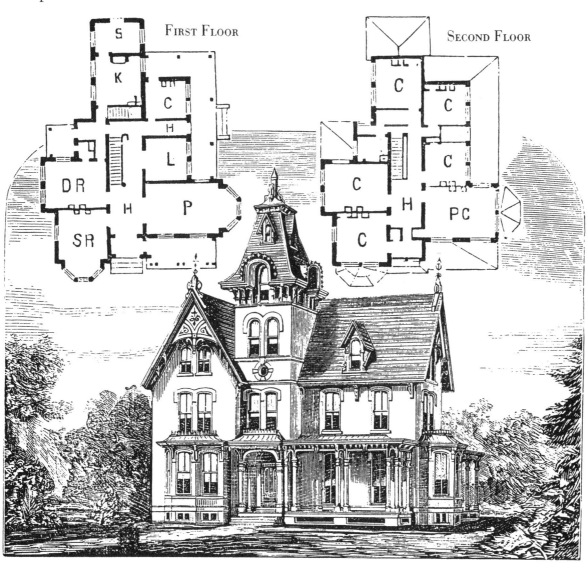

Issac H. Hobbs and Son, Architects, *Hobbs Architecture*, 1873

This is a large, convenient and plain house and well adapted to the requirements of a farm residence, and yet in a farm house it would seem as though of all places this is the one where we should find large fireplaces. These could have been added with very little additional expense, but instead we have what the owner desired, a single flue and walls furred out to make a show of a breast - what we should call a sham.

Mr. Hotchkiss is undoubtedly a modest man, as when he erected his house he left off the front gable and kept the front of the building unbroken, as he was afraid his neighbors would talk if he built something different from what they had. By doing this Mr. Hotchkiss undoubtedly ruined the design and decreased the value of the building at least $500.00, spending his money to please his neighbors.

We have no doubt but what the house will be painted white, although we did not in our specifications call for it to be so, yet it is in keeping with the style of painting in the same locality, and if there is anything to mar the landscape it is this white abomination. We regret to say these things, but feel as though to be perfectly fair to our readers we should state some of the faults in our designs, and give our experiences, so that people who intend to build may avoid falling into these faults.

The veranda is a pleasant feature, and is very useful besides being ornamental; the sitting-room is the finest room in the house, both on account of its size and the view that is obtained from it; the milk room and woodshed, which are necessary appendages to a house of this kind, are located in the rear and are convenient of access from the kitchen and exterior, and are covered with a separate roof, being only

A Farmhouse

The Residence of Dwight Hotchkiss,
Sharon, Connecticut

one story in height. There is a cellar under the whole house built of stone found on the ground. Cost $2,900.00.

Some people will procure plans and specifications and then set their builder to work, being too parsimonious to furnish him with details of construction to enable him to properly carry out the design, and which is a very important matter, as what is the use of getting a good design if it is not to be carried out. Several such cases have come under our notice, and in some instances the builders have obtained details and paid for them, but it is generally the other kind of builders who get such work, and they are apt to estimate with much more liberal figures when they can carry out the designs as they please. One case of this kind in particular, came under our notice, and after the building was completed it did not represent the drawings in any particular except the general form, the design being fearfully butchered and the detail all changed by the builder, who in some instances got the owner's sanction to change, persuading him that what he was going to do would be better, and would cost him, the builder, more, but that he would make no charge to the owner. The house which cost but $1,800, would have been worth $500 more had the design been properly executed. —George and Charles Palliser, Architects, *Palliser's Model Homes*, 1878

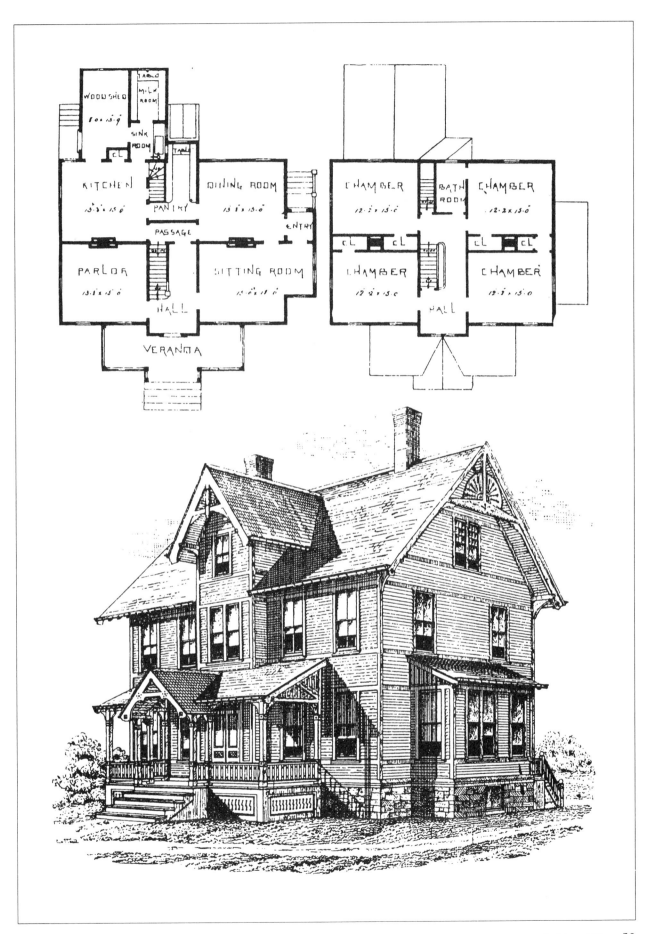

While we have endeavored to concentrate within moderate limits the necessary conveniences of a comfortable mode of living for the occupants, we have not neglected the outward expression of taste that contributes so largely to the pleasure of the beholder. A plain building, by a few, simple, well-directed touches, can thus be invested with a character approaching the ornate. A brief analysis of the design before us will attest the truth of the above remark. Remove first the barge and eave treatment, and we destroy at once the polish of the expression; but take away the pinnacles, and we greatly weaken the expression itself, almost entirely depriving it of that piquancy that strikes us so forcibly in the present view. The analysis might be pushed further, to the consideration of the effect of removing dormers, changing the style of chimney tops, etc.; but we have said enough to show what " Great effects from little causes flow."

Accommodation—The internal arrangement of this dwelling are so plainly exhibited on the plan of the principal floor, as scarcely to need explanation. G is an open entrance porch. A, 8 by 16 feet, is the entrance hall, and contains a flight of stairs. B, 16 by 18 feet is the dining-room, lighted by a recessed twin window, and having an ample china closet attached. The parlor C, 16 by 16 feet, has a nice bay-window, but would be improved by a window extending to the floor on the side next to the entrance porch, an idea not fully conveyed by the engraving. The kitchen D, 16 by 16 feet, is well lighted, and provided with sink, side entrance, and small closet. Adjoining the kitchen there is a wash-house E, 11 by 12 feet, and beyond this a wood-house or pump-room F, 7 by 12 feet, having outdoor communication independent of the kitchen.

Ascending to the second floor, we find the stair landing, marked by the letter H, from which we have ready access to the chambers I

A COTTAGE IN THE RURAL GOTHIC STYLE

and J, and to the bed-room K and bath-room L. The chambers, as will be seen, are all furnished with good closets.

Four small sleeping-rooms, lighted by dormer and gable windows, may be fitted up in the space afforded by the pitch of the roof.

Construction—A very pretty effect would be secured by building this cottage of wood, the weatherboarding being put on in the vertical manner, and the joints battened. The gable and eave cornice should be cut from 3 inch plank, in a bold manner, and also the ornament against the base of the pinnacles.

Samuel Sloan, Architect, *Sloan's Homestead Architecture*, 1866

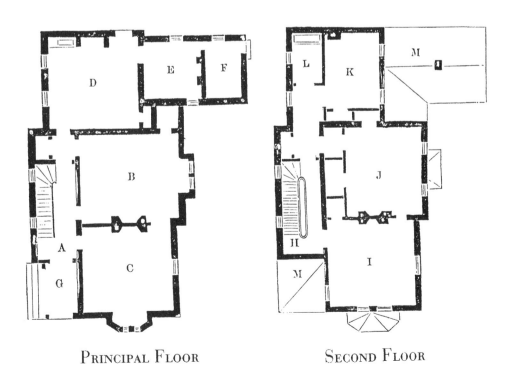

PRINCIPAL FLOOR   SECOND FLOOR

A Cottage

George and Charles Palliser, Architects, *Palliser's Model Homes*, 1878

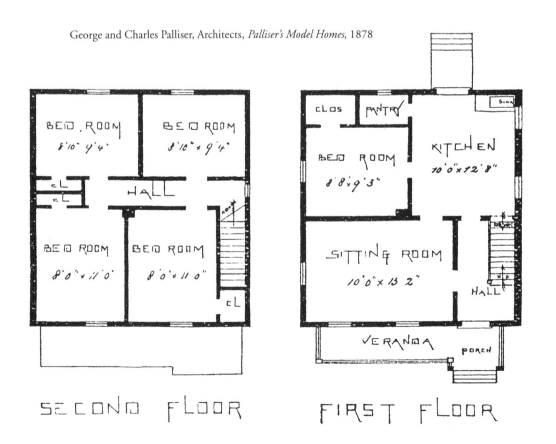

SECOND FLOOR

BED ROOM
8'10" x 9'4"

BED ROOM
8'10" x 9'4"

CL
CL

HALL

BED ROOM
8'0" x 11'0"

BED ROOM
8'0" x 11'0"

CL

FIRST FLOOR

CLOS

PANTRY

SINK

BED ROOM
8'8" x 9'3"

KITCHEN
10'0" x 12'8"

SITTING ROOM
10'0" x 13'2"

HALL

VERANDA

PORCH

This is a good sample of modern buildings now being built throughout the Southern States; it will cost to construct, of frame, about $4000 to $5000; it has a large frontage, and, suitably situated, will produce a fine effect. All of these designs are organized to meet the wants of our customers, and many times we are even held by existing foundations. We are very often furnished by ladies the general disposition of halls, rooms, etc., so that we have merely to make the same practical, so that they can be built, making as few alterations as possible to obtain that result. We rarely, if ever, fail to meet the full wants of families by the adoption of such a course, and know of no buildings failing to please the owner when built, except the price is sometimes above their wants. When so, we alter to suit them.

First Floor: H, hall, 8 feet; P, parlor, 18 feet by 19 feet 6 inches; C, chamber, 16 by 16 feet; C, chamber, 14 by 18 feet; C, chamber, 14 by 18 feet; D-R, dining room, 16 by 18 feet; K, kitchen, 16 by 18 feet. Second Floor. C, chamber, 18 feet by 19 feet 6 inches; C, chamber, 14 by 18 feet; C, chamber, 14 by 18 feet; S R, sitting-room, 16 by 18 feet; B R, bed room, 16 by 18 feet.

AN AMERICAN COTTAGE VILLA

Issac H. Hobbs and Son, Architects, *Hobbs Architecture*, 1873

Irregular in plan and general outline, yet neat and chaste in detail, the design before us is a fair type of the beauty that may be attained without a tendency to extravagance in the exterior adornment of an edifice springing from an irregular basis.

Accommodation—By reference to the plan of the first floor, the internal arrangements will be perceived almost at a glance. The through hall B is entered from the piazza A. This hall contains the stairs, and affords access, by a side passage, to the kitchen E. The parlor C is 15 by 30 feet, and has a rectangular bay-window, communicating by a lengthened window with the veranda I. The dining-room, D, has also a bay-window, seen in the perspective view. F is the butler's pantry, G a woodshed, and H a kitchen closet.

The plan of the second floor exhibits the arrangement of the chambers. K is the landing of the stairs in the front building, from which the three chambers L are entered, and from which also the stairs are continued to the roof-story, in which three very comfortable bedrooms may be fitted up. A passage from the half-landing of the stairs leads to the bathroom M and the adjoining bedroom N, over the kitchen.

This house could be very efficiently warmed by a single furnace, the proximity of the flues being quite favorable to that mode: the hall, parlor, and dining-room, and the three chambers over, could all be kept comfortably warm, as the central position of the flues involves but little loss of heat.

An Irregular Country House

Samuel Sloan, Architect,
Sloan's Homestead Architecture, 1866

Construction—This design admits with equal facility the use of wood or more solid materials. The thickness of walls, as drawn, indicates the use of stone, which, in many districts, is the cheapest material. The pitch of the roof seems to demand shingle or slate; the drawing represents them of varied form.

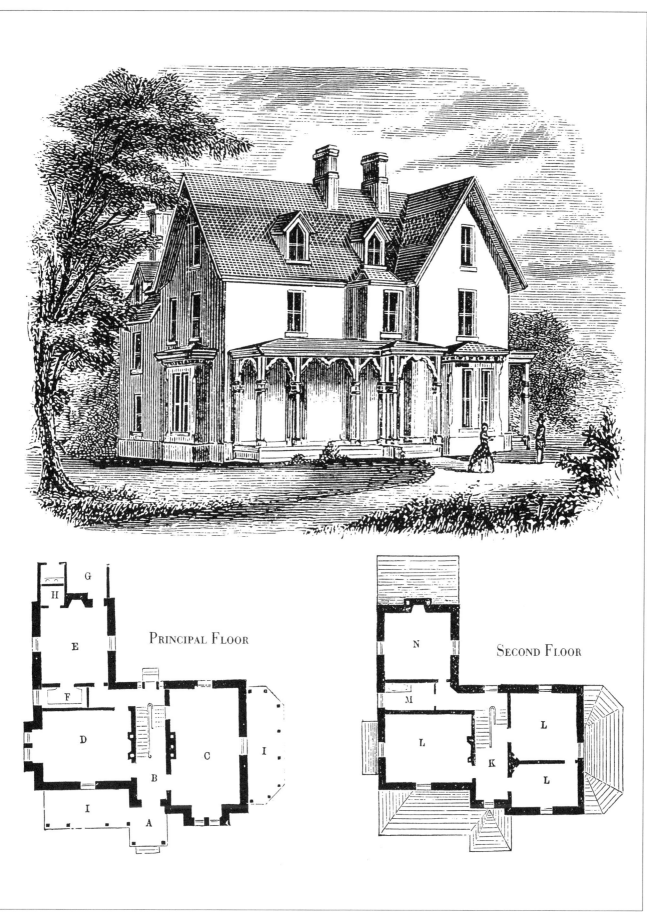

PRINCIPAL FLOOR

SECOND FLOOR

First Floor

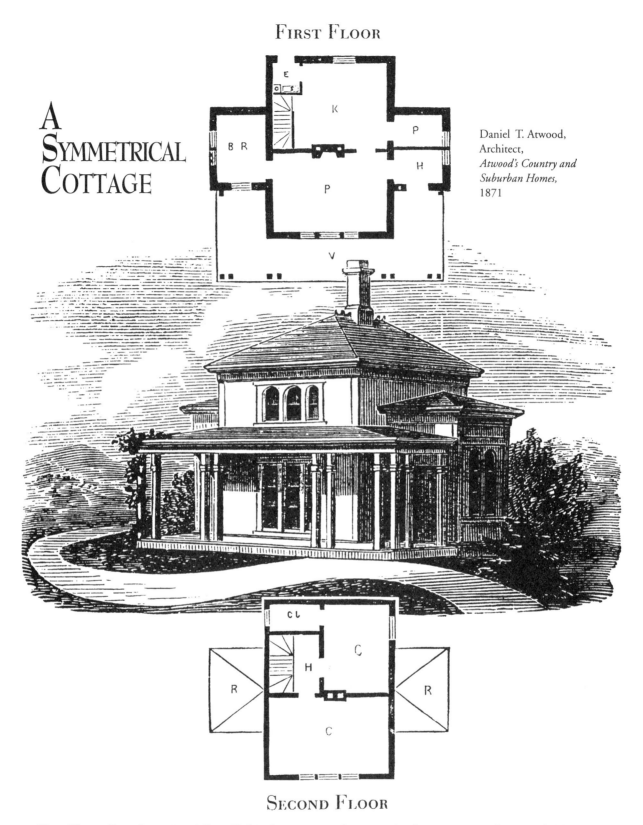

A Symmetrical Cottage

Daniel T. Atwood,
Architect,
*Atwood's Country and
Suburban Homes,*
1871

Second Floor

First Floor: P, parlor, 12x15 feet; K, kitchen, 12x15 feet; BR, bed room, 8x12 feet; H, lobby or entry, 6x8 feet; P, pantry, 6 x 8 feet.

Second Floor: C, two bedrooms, one 12x15 feet, and one 9x12 feet; CL, closet, 4x6 feet; H, hall, 6 feet wide.

A Dwelling House

George E. Woodward, Architect, *Woodward's National Architect*, 1868

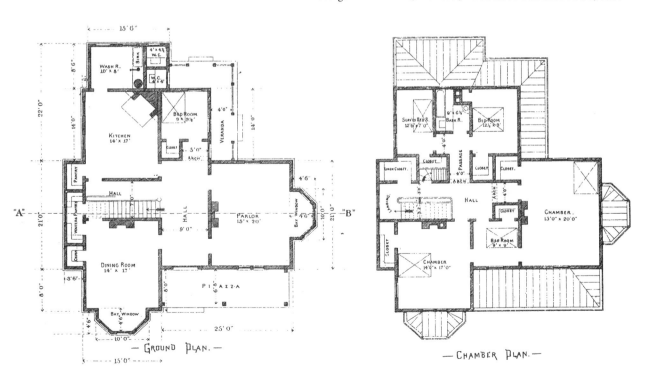

— Ground Plan. —

— Chamber Plan. —

AN IRREGULAR BRACKETED COUNTRY HOME

We might, with almost equal propriety, have termed this a farmhouse. The only objection to this is the probability of impressing the reader with the idea that its application would be accordingly restricted. Indeed, it almost deserves the name of Villa; but the total absence of ostentation in its external aspect inclines us to the appellation we have bestowed upon it, notwithstanding the villa-like extent of its accommodations. Plain, sensible, and solid, it is within the reach and applicable to the circumstances of many who love convenience without ambitious display, and who prefer dignified plainness to gingerbread ostentation. Architecturally, this design aims at being a country dwelling, manifesting the dignity, comfort, and substantial character of social life that is attainable in the country. There is a growing demand for this class of dwellings. Farmers are becoming rich, merchants and manufacturers are retiring from business; and we know that while the frank modesty of the farmer seldom allows him to aspire to towers or pinnacles, nine out of ten of retired citizens are too plain and practical in their views to seek for more than the embodiment of the various accommodations suited to their modes of life, at the lowest grade of expense requisite to give them a tasteful and substantial home. Since we have held these points in view, our motive for the comprehensive appellation "country-house" will be at once perceived.

Accommodation—A veranda G, furnishes the entrance way to the main hall D. A drawing room A, 14 by 26 feet, entered by folding doors from the hall, forms a very interesting portion of this plan, on account of relative situation, its modest little bay window, and the adjoining veranda, which is approached through lengthened windows, and communicates in the same manner with the sitting-room. This sitting-room, marked B, is 22 by 14 feet, and communicates directly with the drawing-room and main hall. This hall is 12 feet square, and a passage, containing the main stairway, leads to the rear entrance, and affords communication with the kitchen and private stairs. An arch thrown over the stair passage, at its junction with the hall D, will give the latter a complete individuality, and will be not only productive of effect as a feature, but gives opportunity for the introduction of a separate and dissimilar cornice, and, in short, establishes for the main hall a character exclusively its own.

A dining-room, 17 by 24 feet, furnished with china closet, and entered from the main hall, is located in the front portion of the house. With the facilities attendant on the mode of service which generally obtains in the style of living of which this house is assumed to be an exponent, all the fixtures of the table can be promptly removed, and the apartment, under the auspices of youthful management, becomes a scene of social and even sportive enjoyment. The private stairs are situated between the dining-room and kitchen, communicating with a small lobby, which is intended for a passage between these apartments. The kitchen E, 14 by 20 feet, is provided with a side entrance, and a very respectable appendage, 12 by 14 feet, which may be used as a pump-shed, wood-house, or bakery. In the latter case a suitable oven will be built, so as to vent its smoke into the kitchen chimney.

By reference to the plan of the second floor, it will be observed that the chambers are respectively designated by the letter H. I is the hall, and K the roofs of verandas. Good bedrooms may be fitted up in the garret, care being taken to provide for their ventilation, in addition to that afforded by gable windows.

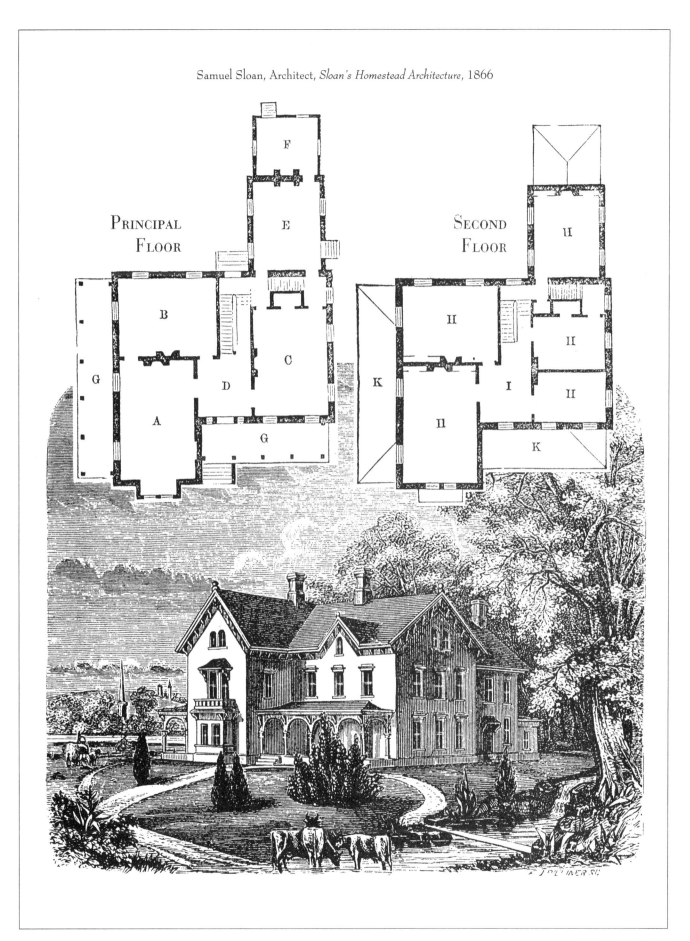

Samuel Sloan, Architect, *Sloan's Homestead Architecture*, 1866

PRINCIPAL
FLOOR

SECOND
FLOOR

Architect George Palliser had a hard time convincing his client to build the house below exactly as designed. The architect complained that farmer W. Coe wanted a house "just after the same idea as others in his locality." Mr. Coe finally built the home, as planned, but painted it white instead of the original high-fashion combination of sage, buff and black.

Palliser felt that "the whole effect was spoiled" by the white paint, but farmer Coe was more concerned with the whole effect of his neighborhood; white paint was the custom. In fact, Palliser's shapes and textures would be dazzling in stark white. The plain paint would also show off the subtle tones of the field stone base and slate roof, and the shadows of the carved details.

The core of the house is a traditional center hall plan. Tacked to that, a front veranda and gable raised to the attic combine to allow a cooling breeze through the hall. Those features also give the home some visual charm and character that traditional houses often lacked. Palliser borrowed the two floor bay window from an 1857 plan book by immigrant architect Calvert Vaux. That detail hints at Vaux's memories of England. The exposed sticks as a decoration at the gable, and the pattern of trim that frame the clapboard walls are simpler versions of the ornament of more fashionable homes of the day. The kitchen ell and its veranda, the raised root cellar and the first floor bedroom show that the plan was fashioned for a farm family.

Palliser called this home "a model farmhouse," not because it was just a design study but because "it will answer in many places for exactly the purpose." His book and his mail-order plans spread this design across the country. Today we can see it as a model too; this the perfect blend of high-style and tradition. It's the joint effort of a farmer and an architect. Because of the mix, we can't fit this home into any of today's categories of architectural style. Yesterday they just called it American.

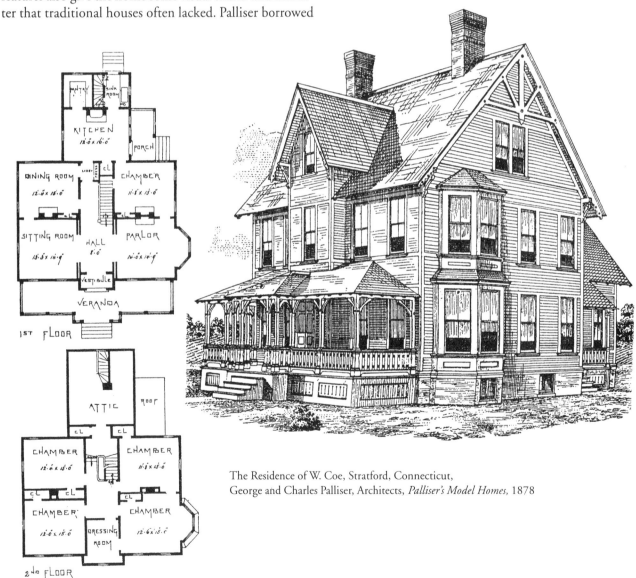

The Residence of W. Coe, Stratford, Connecticut,
George and Charles Palliser, Architects, *Palliser's Model Homes,* 1878

Illustration of a farmhouse veranda used as a summer kitchen from Will Carleton's book *City Ballads*, 1885

Chapter 4

Farmhouses & Farm Cottages
Country Folks' Own Designs

The house is, and always was, the center of American country life. For farmers, it's the family home, the dorm for hired help and the business office. In the eighteenth and nineteenth centuries, it was also an inn for travelers, an infirmary, a textile mill, and a hospice for elderly relatives. The farmhouse kitchen was the factory where fragile raw materials like milk and fruit were turned into durable provisions and saleable products like cheese and preserves.

Farmers considered the barn to be their most valuable building, but that was because the house was not their domain. Farm women managed the household, the kitchen and most of the chores that produced what the family ate and wore. Their work was a never ending cycle, but it could be made more bearable by an efficient, well designed house.

Historian Sally McMurry found that many home plans that had been published in farm journals were designed by farm women and that those designs often took prizes in journal contests and at agricultural society fairs.

Farm wives arranged their homes the same way that their husbands engineered their farmyards. Everything was planned for efficient work and flexibility. Comfort was the next concern. Their plans most often included a kitchen on ground level with a view of the road, a bedroom on the first floor, a cool veranda that could serve as a summer kitchen, good ventilation, and separate accommodations for farm help.

It was important for farmhouses to appear neat and clean, but beyond that, the specific style of the exterior seemed to be of little concern. Many house designs published in farm journals were plans alone, without any exterior view. Farmer William Little of Muscatine, Iowa, sent a home plan to *The Country Gentleman* in 1856 with a note that "it may be built after any of the modern forms."

On the following pages you'll see home designs that seem uninspired compared to the professional designs in Chapter 3. Don't be deceived. The exteriors are simple and almost careless, but the floor plans are creative and well crafted.

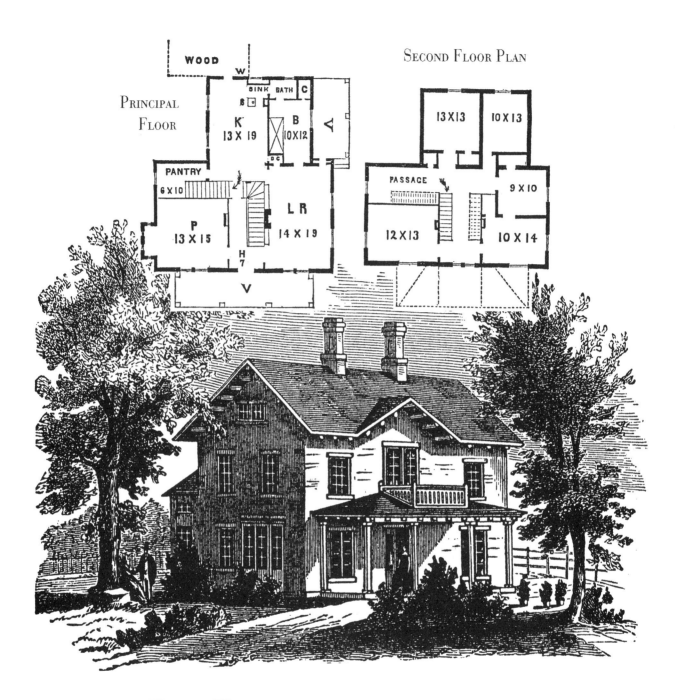

SECOND FLOOR PLAN

PRINCIPAL FLOOR

WOOD

SINK BATH C

K
13 X 19

B
10X12

PANTRY
6 X 10

P
13 X 15

L R
14 X 19

H
7

V

13 X 13

10 X 13

PASSAGE

9 X 10

12 X 13

10 X 14

A BRICK FARM HOUSE

The Register of Rural Affairs, 1859

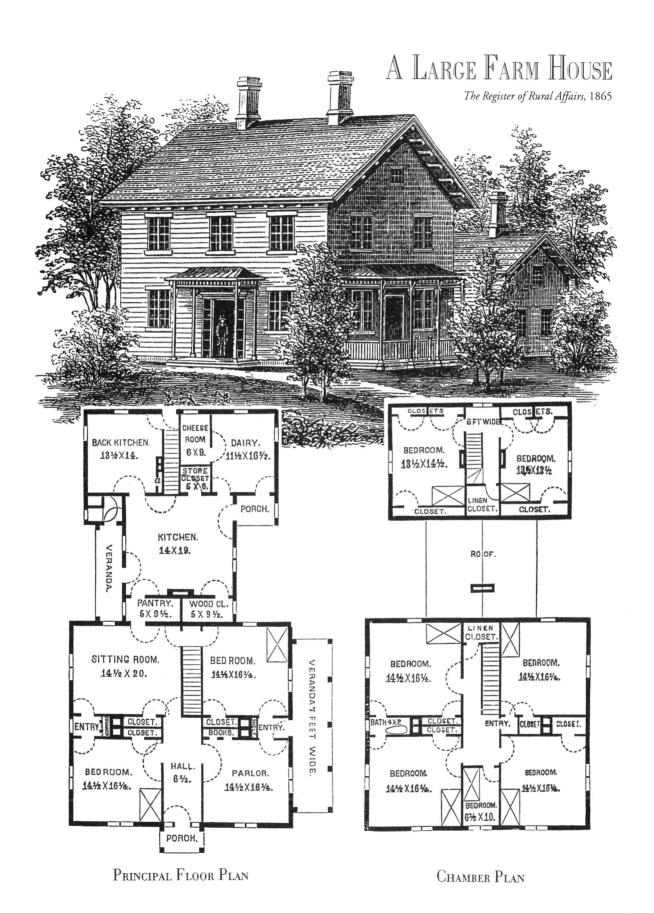

A Large Farm House

The Register of Rural Affairs, 1865

PRINCIPAL FLOOR PLAN

BACK KITCHEN.
13½ X 14.

CHEESE ROOM.
6 X 9.

DAIRY.
11½ X 16½.

STORE CLOSET.
5 X 6.

a

KITCHEN.
14 X 19.

PORCH.

VERANDA.

PANTRY.
5 X 9½.

WOOD CL.
5 X 9½.

SITTING ROOM.
14½ X 20.

BED ROOM.
14½ X 16¼.

ENTRY.

DRAWER

CLOSET.

CLOSET.

CLOSET.

BOOKS.

SHELF

ENTRY.

VERANDA 7 FEET WIDE.

BED ROOM.
14½ X 16¼.

HALL.
6½.

PARLOR.
14½ X 16¼.

PORCH.

CHAMBER PLAN

CLOSETS.

6 FT WIDE

CLOSETS.

BEDROOM.
13½ X 14½.

BEDROOM.
13½ X 13½

CLOSET.

LINEN CLOSET.

CLOSET.

ROOF.

LINEN CLOSET.

BEDROOM.
14½ X 16¼.

BEDROOM.
14½ X 16¼.

BATH 4 X 8

CLOSET.

CLOSET.

ENTRY.

CLOSET.

CLOSET.

BEDROOM.
14½ X 16¼.

BEDROOM.
6½ X 10.

BEDROOM.
14½ X 16¼.

A Bracketed Square House

The Register of Rural Affairs, 1865

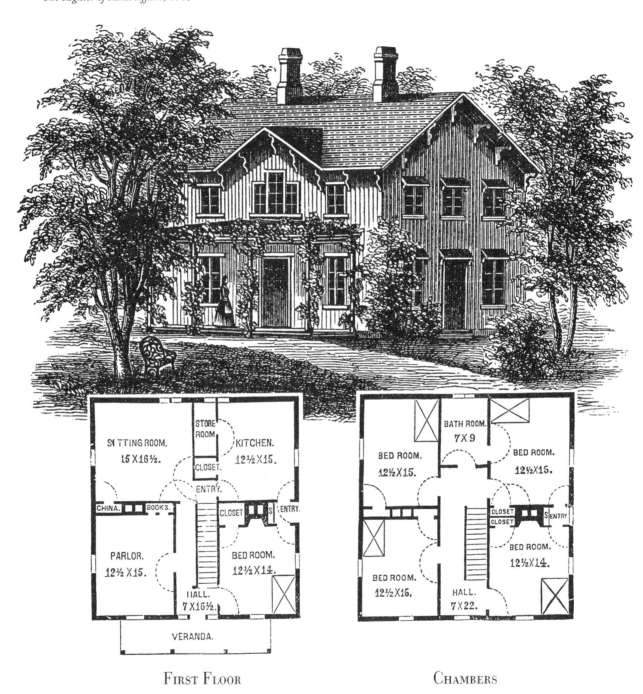

FIRST FLOOR   CHAMBERS

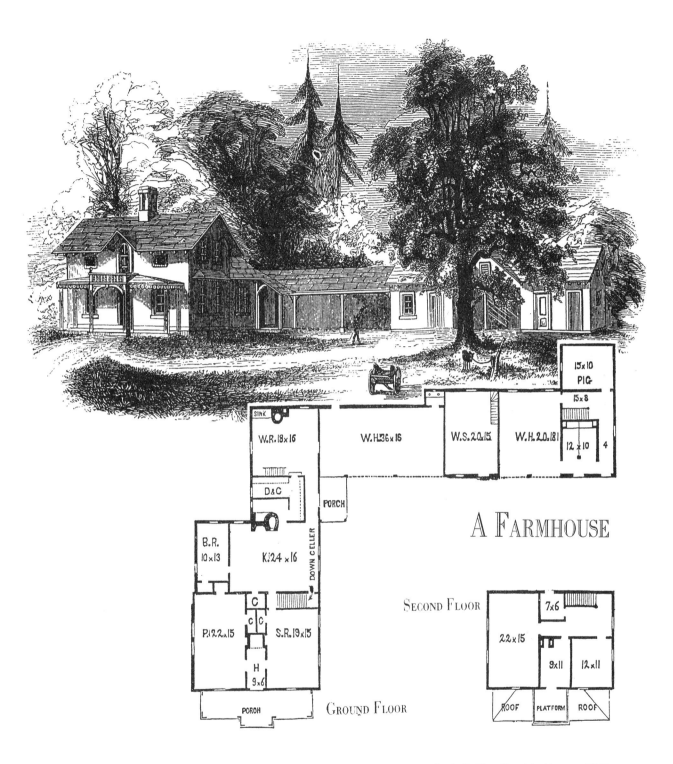

A FARMHOUSE

SECOND FLOOR

GROUND FLOOR

Lewis F. Allen, *Rural Architecture*, 1852

Key: B.R., Bed Room; C, Closets; D&C, Buttery, Dairy and Closet; H, Hall; K, Kitchen; P, Parlor; S.R., Sitting Room; W.R., Wash Room; W.H., Wood House; W.H., Wagon House and Stable; W.S., Work Shed. Second Floor: Chambers.

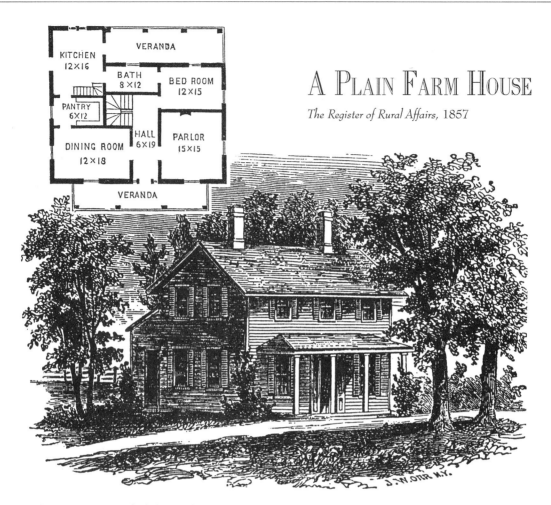

A Plain Farm House

The Register of Rural Affairs, 1857

This design is intended for a farmhouse, where the entire outlay is devoted to convenience and comfort, and not a dollar to mere ornament. It has a special regard to furnishing the greatest amount of room at the least practicable cost.

It will be observed the rooms are compactly disposed, so that those required in connection, are very easily accessible to each other, and no space is lost. The dining room is long and narrow, the most economical form for such an apartment; the kitchen projects in part from the main building, so as to secure a current of air through the opposite doors. The pantry being placed between them, is readily accessible to both, and also affords a passage from one to the other. As personal cleanliness is indispensable to a farmer, a bath is placed between the bedroom (which may be used as nursery,) and the kitchen, for fresh or warm water on one hand, and for dressing on the other. Those who do not need a separate bath room may convert this to a bedroom, or to a milk-room, as circumstances may require. The cellar is reached by a descent placed under the kitchen stairs. The arrangement of the second story is an exact copy of the lower, affording four bedrooms opening into the upper hall; and two more for hired persons, over the pantry and kitchen, and entered by the kitchen stairs. Closets for the rooms may be taken off the front of them, on the outer sides, where the roof is lowest.

It will be observed that this house, although but little more than a story and a half, and twenty-eight by forty feet outside, furnishes no less than twelve rooms besides the hall, closets and cellar—a large amount for the cost. Those to whom the exterior appears plain and destitute of ornament, will supply the deficiency by handsomely planted and neatly kept grounds, a mode, beyond all comparison, the cheapest and most satisfactory, for ornamenting country dwellings.

Plan of a Small House

In this plan I did not extend the hall further than the foot of the stairs, in order to make my stairs wider, and diminish considerably their cost. In the three rooms so well connected—the living-room, the dining room, and the kitchen—are transacted all the business of a house; the housekeeper can give her orders and see them executed, almost without leaving her room. To visitors and strangers I assign the front door, which will take them to any apartment except to the sanctum sanctorum, or the kitchen. Under the stairs can be made closets for the two rooms, right and left. Easy steps lead up stairs to a hall which forms the center of four rooms; the closets on each side of the hall will also be found convenient for the general use of the house. The closet in the central room above will add to its comfort.

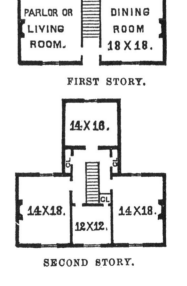

H. Huffman, Richland County, IL.,
The Country Gentleman, 1858
and *The Register of Rural Affairs*, 1859

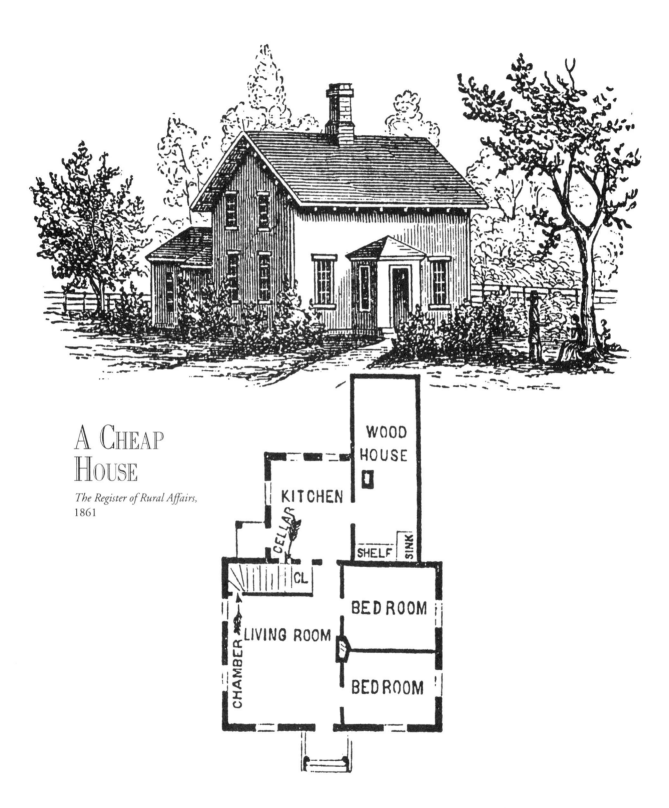

A Cheap House

The Register of Rural Affairs,
1861

WOOD HOUSE

KITCHEN

CELLAR

SHELF | SINK

CL

CHAMBER | LIVING ROOM

BEDROOM

BEDROOM

FIRST FLOOR PLAN

A Farmer's Cottage

L.D. Snook Residence, Yates County, New York

Moore's Rural New Yorker, 1869; *How to Build Furnish & Decorate*, 1883; and *Todd's Country Homes*, 1888

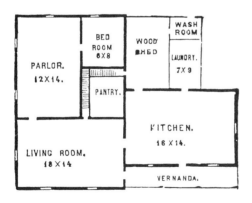

DESIGN 1 - FIRST FLOOR PLAN   DESIGN 2 - FIRST FLOOR PLAN

Two plans for the first floor are here given, as many do not care for a parlor. The kitchen and living room are placed in the front of the house, as there is no good reason why the housewife, in her daily round of duties, should be secluded and shut out from the little variety and amusement derived from a sight of highway travel.

RULES FOR PLANNING, DESIGNING & BUILDING

The Register of Rural Affairs, 1855, 1856 & 1857

The art of planning farmhouses, like that of subdividing farms, should be reduced to a regular system. It is most commonly a mere chance process—a sort of hap-hazard arrangement of rooms, doors and entries, without the observance of any general rules.

After a greater or less number of rooms has been fixed upon, according to wants and circumstances, the next step is to arrange them in the most convenient and economical manner. This is a difficult task to a person of inexperience, but may be greatly assisted by observing the following rules, and by the examination of published plans.

1. Always compare the cost with the means, before deciding on the plan. It is much better to build within means, than to have a large, fine house, hard to keep in order, and encumbering the owner with a heavy and annoying debt. A great error with many is an attempt to build finely. Attend to real wants and substantial conveniences, and avoid imaginary and manufactured desires.

2. Study a convenient location rather than a showy one: a house on a lofty hill may make a fine appearance, but the annoyance of ascending to it will become greater on each successive day.

3. Build of such good materials as are near at hand. An interesting index is thus afforded to the resources and materials of that particular region, with the addition of great economy over the use of such as are "far brought and dear bought."

4. Prefer lasting to perishable materials, even if more costly. A small well built erection, is better than a large decaying shell.

5. Discard all gingerbread work, and adopt a plain, neat, and tasteful appearance in every part. Far more true taste is evinced by proper forms and just proportions than by any amount of tinsel and peacock decorations. A marble statue bedizened with feathers and ribbons, would not be a very pleasing object.

6. Proportion may be shown in the smallest cottage as well as in the most magnificent palace —and the former should be carefully designed as well as the latter. However small a building may be, let it never show an awkward conception, when a good form is more easily made than a bad one.

7. Where convenient or practicable, let the plan be so devised that additions may be subsequently made, without distorting the whole.

8. More attention should be given to the convenient arrangement and disposition of rooms in constant daily use, than those employed but a few times in the course of a year. Hence the kitch-

en and living-room should receive special attention.

9. In all country houses, from the cottage to the palace, let the kitchen (the most important apartment,) always be on a level with the main floor. It requires more force to raise a hundred pounds ten feet upwards, whether it be the human frame or an assortment of eatables, than the same weight one hundred feet on a level. To do it fifty times a day is a serious task. If the mistress superintends her own kitchen, it should be of easy access. For strong light and free ventilation, it should have, if possible, windows on opposite or nearly opposite sides.

10. There should be a set of easy stairs from the kitchen to the cellar. Every cellar should have, besides the stairs within, an outside entrance, for the passage of barrels and other heavy articles.

11. The pantry, and more especially the china closet, should be between the kitchen and dining room for easy access from both.

12. The bathroom should be between the kitchen and nursery, for convenience to warm water.

13. Let the entry or hall be near the center of the house, so that ready and convenient access may be had from it to the different rooms; and to prevent the too common evil of passing through one room to enter another.

14. Place the stairs so that the landing shall be as near the center as may be practicable, for the reasons given in the preceding rule.

15. Every entrance from without, except to the kitchen, should open into some entry, lobby, or hall, to prevent the direct ingress of cold air into rooms, and to secure sufficient privacy.

16. Let the partitions of the second floor stand over those of the lower, as nearly as possible, to secure firmness and stability.

17. The first floor of any house, however small, should be at least one foot above ground, to guard against dampness.

18. Flat roofs should be adopted only with metallic covering. Shingles need a steeper inclination to prevent the accumulation of snow, leakage and decay—more so than is frequently adopted. A steep roof is, additionally, cheaper, by admitting the use of a less perfect material for an equally perfect roof, and giving more garret room.

19. The coolest rooms in summer, and the warmest in winter, are those remote from the direction of the prevailing winds and from the afternoon sun. Hence parlors, nurseries, and other apartments where personal comfort is important, should be placed on this side of the house where practicable.

20. Always reserve ten per cent. of cost for improvement and planting. Remember that a hundred dollars in trees and shrubbery produce a greater ornamental and pleasing effect than a thousand in architecture.

21. Lastly, never build in a hurry; mature plans thoroughly; procure the best materials, and have joiner-work done at the cheaper season of winter, and the erection will be completed in the most perfect manner, and with the greatest practicable degree of economy.

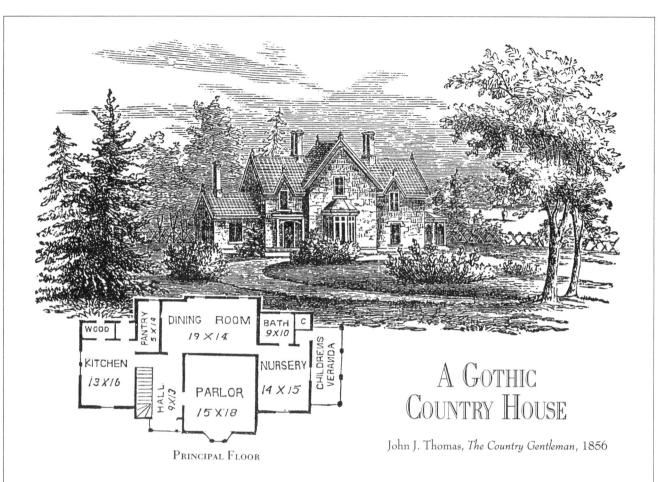

PRINCIPAL FLOOR

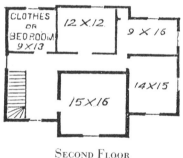

SECOND FLOOR

A GOTHIC COUNTRY HOUSE

John J. Thomas, *The Country Gentleman*, 1856

In order to avoid the fault of the common gothic cottages, seen in all parts of the country, namely a profusion of flimsy ornamental carvings, we present the above view of a simple, well proportioned, and sufficiently tasteful country residence, which may be afforded by most farmers in comfortable circumstances. It need not cost, if built of stone or brick, more than twenty five hundred dollars; and with wood, eighteen to twenty hundred might be sufficient for its completion.

Its exterior needs very little description. There is little or nothing about it which is added purely for ornament, and this materially lessens the expense of erection. The steepness of the roofs prevents danger of leakage at the receding angles, while this quality is not too glaring to detract from its neatness.

From the hall, or entrance, ready access is had to the parlor, dining room, and kitchen, while the latter is rendered less conspicuous by the intervening stairs. The dining room is longer and narrower than common, a more convenient form for its usual purpose; it is, of course, intended in this moderate plan to serve as a family or ordinary living room. The bath room may be used, if desired as a children's bedroom. It will be observed that special attention is given to the comfort of children, by providing them with a pleasant veranda, instead of attaching it to the parlor, a room far less frequently used and used too by those who can well forego a little comfort for a most interesting class of the human race, quite as much deserving, but too often thrust aside to make room for full-grown loungers.

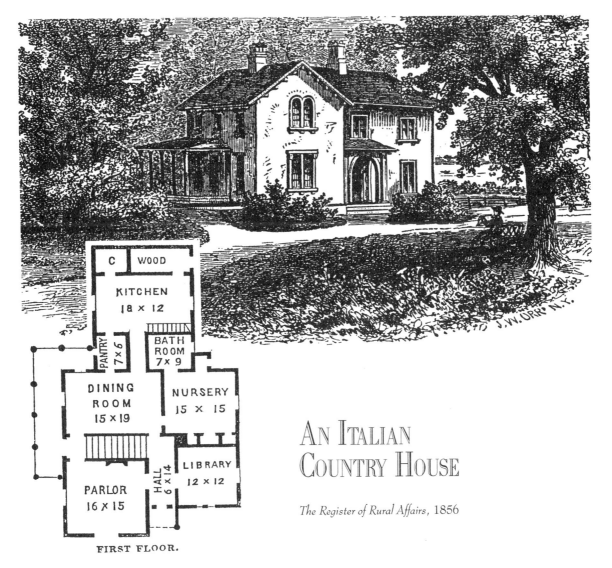

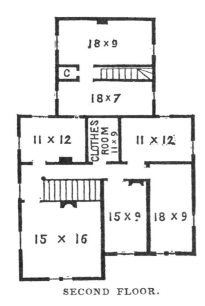

FIRST FLOOR.

C WOOD

KITCHEN
18 × 12

PANTRY
7 × 6

BATH
ROOM
7 × 9

DINING
ROOM
15 × 19

NURSERY
15 × 15

HALL
6 × 14

LIBRARY
12 × 12

PARLOR
16 × 15

SECOND FLOOR.

18 × 9

C

18 × 7

11 × 12

CLOTHES
ROOM
11 × 9

11 × 12

15 × 16

15 × 9

18 × 9

An Italian Country House

The Register of Rural Affairs, 1856

The design here given represents a country residence which contains nearly all the essential comforts for a family residing on a farm, at less cost than a large portion of the heavy built pseudo-Grecian farm houses. The exterior indicates entire simplicity, with a sufficient degree of architectural character, and the interior is a combination of convenience and compactness.

A Prize Winning Farmhouse Plan

The accompanying plan is designed to front south, with an elevation of thirteen feet from the sills to the roof. It should occupy somewhat elevated ground, sloping a little to the north, and should be raised on an underpinning to suit the ground. To give chambers to the size designated, the apex of the roof should be not less than twenty-two or twenty-three feet above the sills. It is highly proper to leave a space for air, between the finish of the chambers and the roof, which will prevent the rooms from becoming heated in summer.

The site should be selected with the view to the easy construction of drains from the sinks, bathing house, dairy, &c. directly to the piggery or barn yard.

It is of course expected a good farmer will have a good cellar and in some situations, the best way of warming a house is by a hot air furnace in the cellar. The size of the cellar and its particular divisions, should of course depend on the wants or circumstances of the builders. In some cases it may be expedient to have it extend under the whole of the main body of the house.

It may be observed, however, that it is not advisable to store large quantities of vegetables under dwellings, as the exhalations from them, especially when unsound, are known to be decidedly prejudicial to health. Hence the barn cellar, and not that of the dwelling house, should be the repository of such vegetables as are wanted for the use of domestic animals.

In the construction of this plan, it has been my object to combine utility and beauty, as far as practical with the labor-saving principal. In the arrangement of the kitchen and dairy, particularly, special regard has been had to securing the proper requisites for those important departments with the greatest practicable degree of convenience.

In constructing a dairy, it is proper that such an excavation should be made as will leave the floor, which should be made of stones, two or three feet below the surrounding surface. The sides should be of brick or stone, and plastered; the walls high, and the windows made so as to shut out the light and admit the air. The advantage of thorough ventilation and pure air is acknowledged by every one who has ever paid attention to the manufacture of butter, though it is a matter generally too little thought of, in the construction of apartments for this purpose. It will be observed, that in the plan herewith submitted, an open space of two-and-a-half feet has been provided for on three sides of the dairy.

To render the establishment as perfect as possible, the command of a good spring of water, which may be conducted through the dairy-room, is necessary; when that cannot be had, an ice house in direct contact, (as in the accompanying plan,) and a good well of water convenient, form the best substitute.

The expense of such a house in this vicinity might be varied from fifteen hundred to three thousand dollars; according to the style of finish, the taste and ability of the owner, &c. The main conveniences may be retained at the lowest estimate, by omitting the ornamental front.

Farmers won awards for their home and barn designs just as they did for huge pumpkins and prize pigs. Farm journals and local agricultural societies ran frequent contests. Matilda W. Howard, of Zanesville, Ohio, won the prize given by the Committee on Farm Dwellings at the 1848 meeting of the New York State Agricultural Society. The editors of *The Cultivator* published her plan in their August, 1850, issue. They added the engraving of how the home might appear when built.

Historian Sally McMurry found another design by Mrs. Howard in a 1843 issue of *The Cultivator*. With that plan the designer explained her architectural apprenticeship as "six years' residence in a farm house which . . . was very defective."

Ohio farmer Matilda W. Howard's farmhouse plan, shown with a suggested exterior design.
The Cultivator, 1850

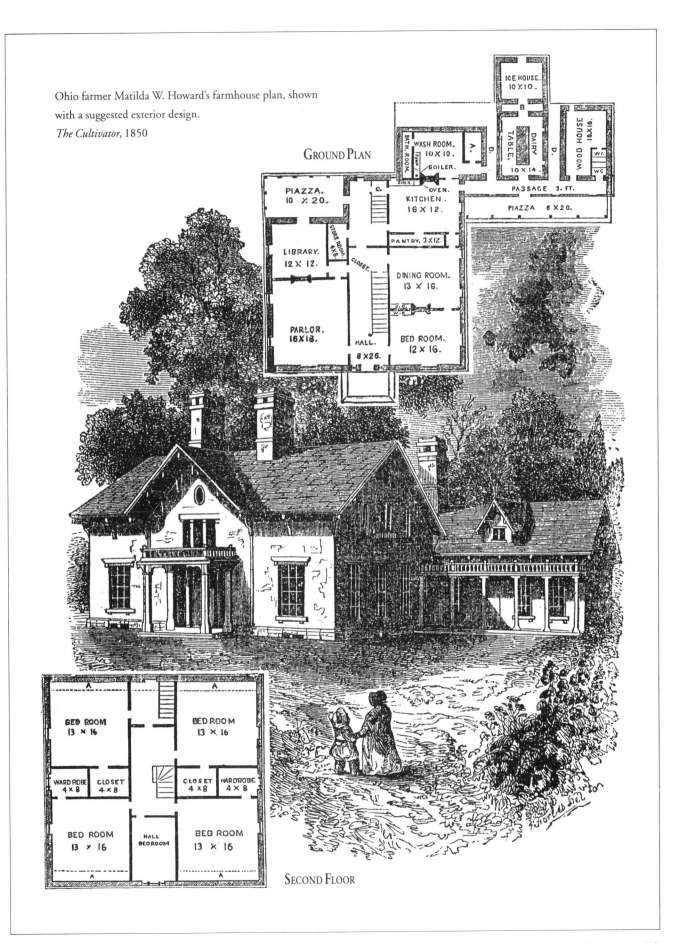

GROUND PLAN

SECOND FLOOR

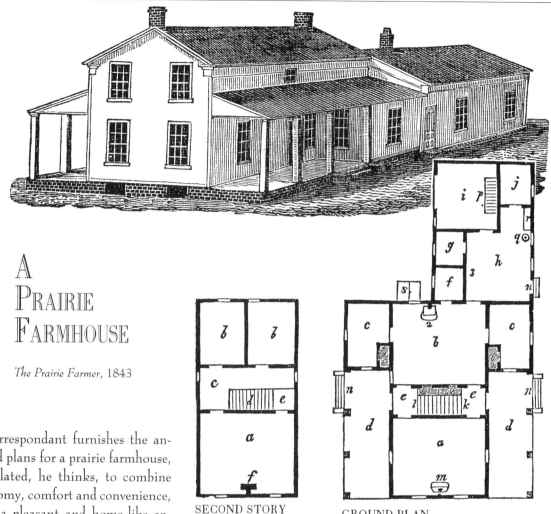

A Prairie Farmhouse

The Prairie Farmer, 1843

SECOND STORY

GROUND PLAN

A correspondant furnishes the annexed plans for a prairie farmhouse, calculated, he thinks, to combine economy, comfort and convenience, with a pleasant and home-like appearance.

It is designed for a southern or eastern aspect, the end fronting on the road. The plan is drawn for a frame house, but may be altered for brick or stone by increasing the thickness of the walls. Its convenience will be seen at a glance. It contains all the room which the farmer of moderate circumstances needs, and there is none that is superfluous. Should any like to build after the plan, who are not able to build the whole at once, the rear part can be put up first, and will answer as a dwelling, by using the meal room as a bed room. The main building is 18 by 36 feet, outside; the lean-to additions, each 8 feet wide. The rear building is 18 by 25 feet. The posts to the main building are 16 feet; to the piazzas, 10 feet; to the rear building, 12 feet. The rooms of the lower floor are 9 feet between floors, the chambers, 8 feet. The room b. is intended for a dining room in summer, and the room h. for a summer kitchen. In winter, the room b. is to be used for both purposes. The expense of completing the whole, including a cellar under the main part, is estimated at from $800 to $1,000, according to the location and material used.

Ground Plan: a, Parlor, 17x15 feet; b, Kitchen and Dining Room; c,c, Bed Rooms, 8x13 feet; d, Piazzas, 8x23 feet; e,e, Entries, 6 feet wide; f, Buttery, 6 feet square; g, Milk Room, 6 feet square; h, Back Kitchen, 12x13 feet; i, Wood House, 12 feet square; j, Meal Room, 6x8 feet; k, Chamber Stairs, 4 feet wide; l, Cellar Stairs; m, Franklin Stove; n,n,n, Steps; o,o,o,o, Closets; p, Wood House Stairs: q, Pump; r, Sink; s, Bulkhead, covering outside cellar stairs; 2, Cooking Stove; 3, Place for Stove in summer.

Second Story: a, Chamber, 17x15 feet; b,b, Bed Rooms, 12x18 feet; c, Passage; d, Staircase; e, Closet; f, Drum connected by pipe with stove below.

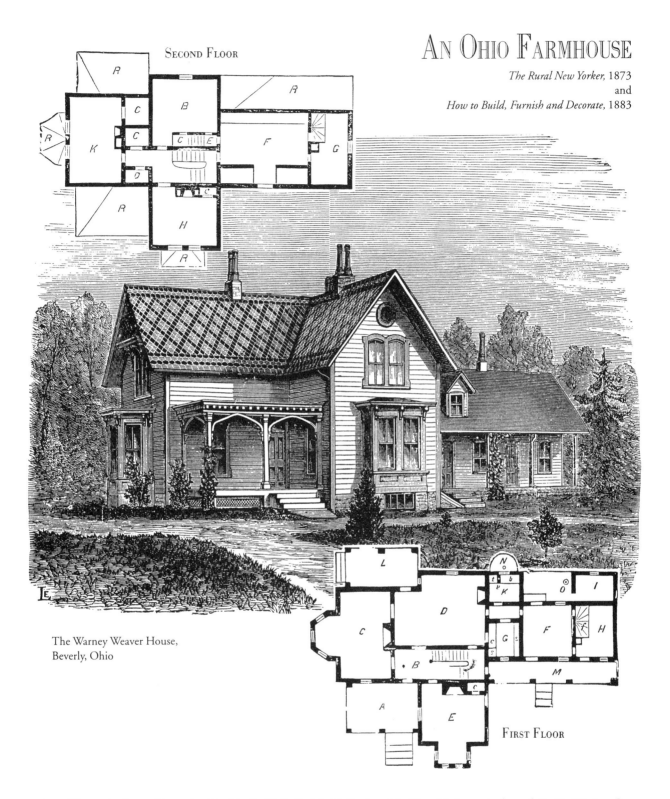

SECOND FLOOR

AN OHIO FARMHOUSE

The Rural New Yorker, 1873
and
How to Build, Furnish and Decorate, 1883

The Warney Weaver House,
Beverly, Ohio

FIRST FLOOR

First Floor: A, Front Veranda, 10x16; B, Hall, 7x20; C, Parlor, 12x18, with bay window, 4x9; D, Dining Room, 15x20; E, Library, 12x15, with square bay window, 4x8; F, Kitchen, 11x12; G, Pantry, 8x8; H, Store Room, 10x12; I, Coal Room, 7.5x8; K, Wash Room, 7.5x8; L, Veranda, 8x16; M, Veranda, 4x30; N, Cistern, 9 feet diameter; O, Well; c,c, Closets; s,s, Shelves; b, Bath; f, Back Stairs; t, Sink; p, Pump.

Second Floor: Hall, 7 feet wide; C,C,C,C, Closets; B, Bed Room, 15x15; D, Linen Closet; E, Attic Stairs; F, Servants' Bed Room, 11x20; G, Garret; H, Bed Room, 12x15; K, Bed Room, 12x16.

The Style of Farm Buildings

Lewis F. Allen, *Rural Architecture*, 1852

We are quite aware that different forms or fashions of detail and finish, to both outside and inside work, prevail among builders in different sections of the United States. Some of these fashions are the result of climate, some of conventional taste, and some of education. With them we are not disposed to quarrel. In many cases they are immaterial to the main objects of the work, and so long as they please the taste or partialities of those adopting them, are of little consequence.

We are no professional builder, and of course free from the dogmas which are too apt to be inculcated in the professional schools and workshops. We give a wide berth, and a free toleration in all such matters, and are not disposed to raise a hornet's nest about our ears by interfering in matters where every tyro of the drafting board and work-bench assumes to be, and probably may be, our superior. All minor subjects we are free to leave to the skill and ingenuity of the builder who, fortunately for the country, is found in almost every village and hamlet of the land.

Modes and styles of finish, both inside and outside of buildings change; and that so frequently, that what is laid down as the reigning fashion today, may be superseded by another fashion of tomorrow—immaterial in themselves, and not affecting the shape, arrangement, and accommodation of the building itself.

As a general remark, all buildings should show for themselves, what they are built of. Let stone be stone; bricks show on their own account; and of all things, put no counterfeit by way of plaster, stucco, or other false pretense other than paint, or a durable wash upon wood: it is a miserable affectation always, and of no possible use whatever.

The character of the farm should be carried out so as to express itself in everything which it contains. All should bear a consistent relation with each other. The farmer himself is a plain man. His family are plain people, although none the less worthy, useful, or exalted, on that account. His structures, of every kind, should be plain, also, yet substantial, where substance is required. All these detract nothing from his respectability or his influence in the neighborhood, the town, the county, or the state. A farmer has quite as much business in the field, or about his ordinary occupations, with ragged garments, out at elbows, and a crownless hat, as he has to occupy a leaky, wind-broken, and dilapidated house. Neither is he any nearer the mark, with a ruffled shirt, a fancy dress, or gloved hands, when following his plough behind a pair of fancy horses, than in living in a finical, pretending house, such as we see stuck up in conspicuous places in many parts of the country.

Key to the Farmhouse Plans on Page 83:

Ground Floor: BR, Bed Room; DR, Dining Room; DC, Dining Closet; D, Dairy ; H, Hall; P, Parlor; SR, Sitting Room; WR, Wash Room with Bathing Room and B, Bedroom for a hired man; WH, Wood House; WS, Work Shed. The 16x18 room at the front left of the Ground Floor is a Library. The 12x8 room off that is a farm Office with its own entrance. The 20x15 room that opens off the side veranda is the Kitchen.

Second Floor: the 26x12 space is the upper Hall. All other rooms with dimensions are Chambers. The unlabled spaces are closets.

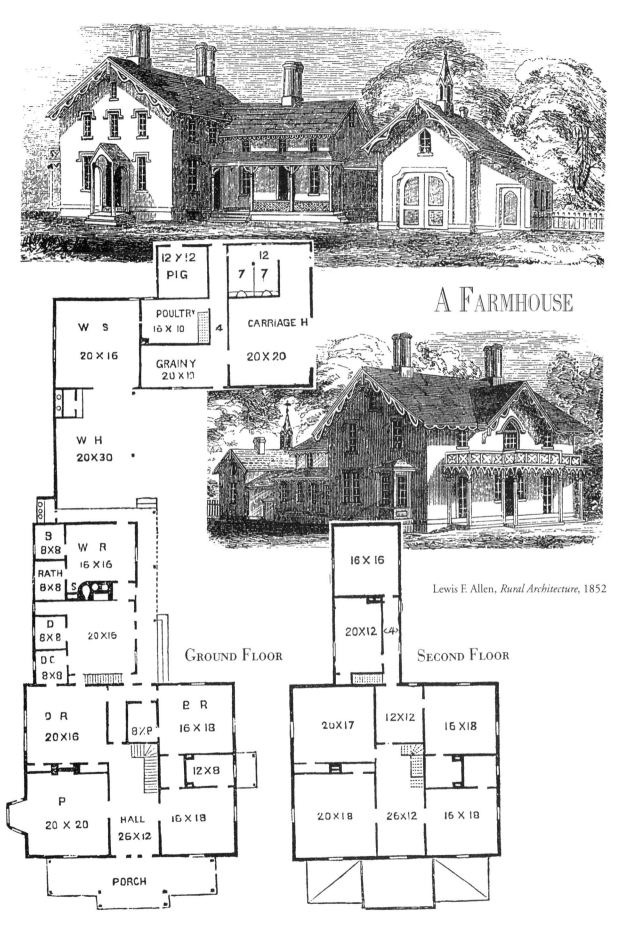

A FARMHOUSE

Lewis F. Allen, *Rural Architecture*, 1852

GROUND FLOOR

SECOND FLOOR

PIG 12 ✗ 12

POULTRY 16 X 10

GRAIN Y 20 X 10

12

7 7

4

CARRIAGE H 20 X 20

W S 20 X 16

W H 20 X 30

B 8 X 8

W R 16 X 16

RATH 8 X 8

S

D 8 X 8

D C. 8 X 8

20 X 15

D R 20 X 16

8 X 8

2 R 16 X 18

12 X 8

P 20 X 20

HALL 26 X 12

16 X 18

PORCH

16 X 16

20 X 12

4

20 X 17

12 X 12

16 X 18

20 X 18

26 X 12

16 X 18

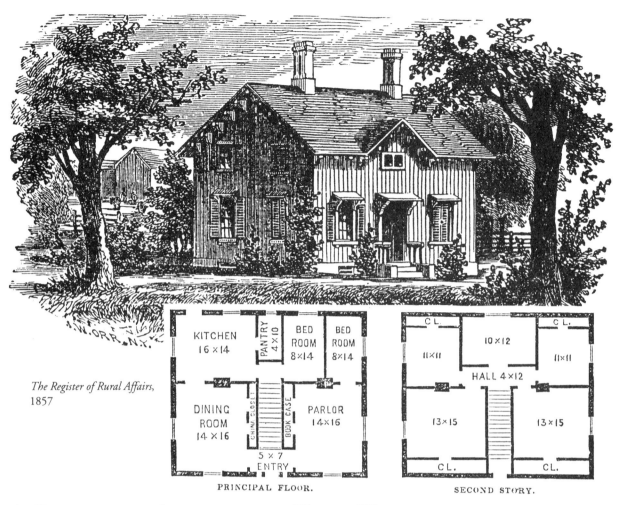

KITCHEN 16 × 14

PANTRY 4×10

BED ROOM 8×14

BED ROOM 8×14

DINING ROOM 14 × 16

CHINA CLOSET

BOOK CASE

PARLOR 14×16

5 × 7 ENTRY

PRINCIPAL FLOOR.

CL.

10 × 12

CL.

11×11

11×11

HALL 4×12

13 × 15

13 × 15

CL.

CL.

SECOND STORY.

The Register of Rural Affairs,
1857

A BRACKETED SYMMETRICAL FARM HOUSE

This 1857 farmhouse design adopted the bracketed style from architect A.J. Downing's earlier publications. It changes Downing's concept of a decorative cottage for estate workers into a heart-of-the-farm house with a higher, more usable second floor and practical details like shutters, common window sash, and a raised, ventilated cellar. Where the professional designer set his cottage in an exotic-looking landscape, the farmer has his set square with his barns and fronted by common shade trees.

A Model Workingman's Cottage
A.J. Downing, Architect
The Horticulturist, 1847
and
The Architecture of Country Houses,
1850

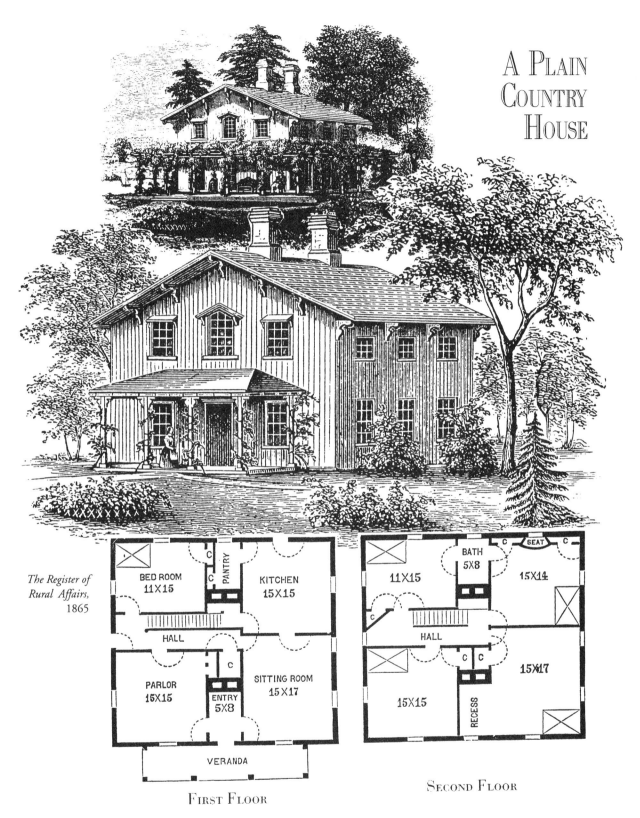

A PLAIN COUNTRY HOUSE

The Register of Rural Affairs, 1865

First Floor

BED ROOM 11×15
PANTRY
KITCHEN 15×15
HALL
PARLOR 15×15
ENTRY 5×8
SITTING ROOM 15×17
VERANDA

Second Floor

11×15
BATH 5×8
SEAT
15×14
HALL
15×15
RECESS
15×17

The design of a house with an arbor-veranda, from A.J. Downing's book *The Architecture of Country Houses* is shown at the top. The farm journal design that it inspired might look a bit less graceful, but it has a far more usable layout. Downing's house had a cellar kitchen, very small bedrooms without closets and a wastefully big parlor. The plan, above, is elegant in its efficiency.

Farm Cottages

While a great interest has been felt in the improvement of the better class of country dwellings, the cheaper farm houses and workingmen's cottages, have been much neglected. Yet we venture the assertion, that more of the comfort and success of country living, and more of the prosperity of farming generally, depends on the erection of laborers' cottages, than on all other dwellings put together. This we propose to show.

In the first place, farming has been regarded to a great extent by those who judge merely from the outside appearance, as an inseparable bar to respectability. Foolish as this notion may seem, it has not been without its cause; and farmers themselves are in some measure to blame for it. They have not attended sufficiently to the cultivation of rural taste. They have not studied to make their homes pleasant and attractive by ornamental planting, gardening, fruit raising; by neat, well-furnished dwellings, amply provided with literary and scientific food—and too many who have aimed a notch higher than the rest, have rather sought for splendid emptiness, than compact and rural comfort. No wonder then, that farmers' sons so often turn away from what seems so dull and repulsive, and throng the "learned professions."

Another great drawback on the comforts and attractions of country life, is the incessant drudgery to which farmers' wives are generally subjected. The owner and occupant of a large farm must hire several men, and the farmer thinks it cheapest to board and lodge them in his family. There are a few "hired men" that are neat, respectable and intelligent; but the great mass care little for either cleanliness or mental culture. They throng the farmhouse at noon and in the evenings, and often on the Sabbath, so that the wife and daughters have little or no seclusion for conversation, study, or writing, for it is next to impossible to prevent in an ordinary farmhouse a pretty thorough intermixture of individuals of all sorts and sizes. In addition to the inconvenience of this unwelcome occupance, there is still another of serious magnitude—in the amount of drudgery they are compelled to perform in feeding so large and hungry a family. There are many farmers' wives and daughters, although amply provided with property, whose time is closely occupied from earliest dawn till long after dark, with a constant and laborious round of baking, boiling, stewing and roasting—and roasting, stewing, boiling and baking—of washing, scrubbing, ironing, and an endless routine of other labors. It is no wonder, then, that we so often see country women bent down and furrowed with premature old age, while the merchants' and mechanics' wives, and the city resident, who are free from this grinding burden, remain at the same period of life, straight, vigorous, blooming and active. We have heard a most worthy and intelligent woman, who at fifty looked old enough for seventy, remark that at a fair estimate she had cooked at least fifty tons of food for laboring men. This fully explains the reason that town ladies regard it as a sort of state prison punishment to marry young farmers.

Now, remove these two great evils—the slavery of country women—and the repulsive aspect of farming to young men, resulting mainly from this slavery—and a striking revolution would be instantly made in the comfort, respectability, and success of farming. But how is this to be done? The mode is cheap, obvious and simple, - merely by the erection of good laborers' cottages. We have tried this system for many years, and "we know whereof we affirm." Hire married men, who can board at home, and give the farmer's family the exclusive occupancy of their own house and table. Such men can board themselves more cheaply than another can do it, by purchasing just such articles as suits their wants and rules of economy, which are prepared at home at no cost. The farmer, by agreement, may furnish these supplies from his farm. "We cannot get such men as are worth a straw!" exclaims some one who has only provided comfortless shanties for them, into which no smart decent man would thrust his family; but let neat, commodious and tasteful cottages be built, ornamented with a little door-yard shrubbery or mantled with climbing roses and honeysuckles, and no difficulty will be found in getting men of the right stamp. Houses of this character may be built for one hundred and fifty to two hundred dollars each, and will be worth at least one thousand dollars to the man who places any proper estimate on the life and health of his wife. —*The Register of Rural Affairs*, 1855

A Cottage

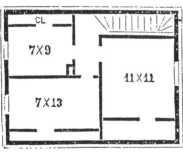

A Small but Complete Cottage

The Register of Rural Affairs, 1881

The Register of Rural Affairs, 1861

Plan

W. H.

LIVING ROOM
12 X 17

BED ROOM
7 X 9

CL
7 X 9

7 X 13

11 X 11

Bedrooms

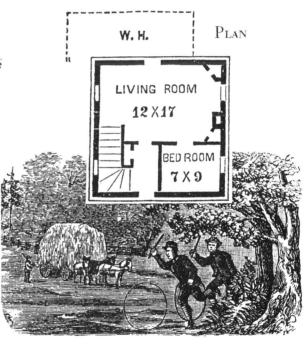

BEDROOM
9 X 9

BEDROOM
9 X 9

TO CELLAR

LIVING ROOM
15 X 18

TO CHAMBER

Principal Floor

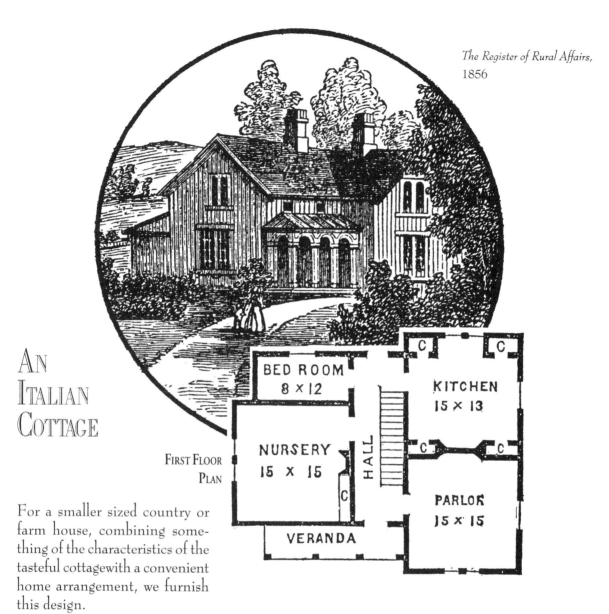

The Register of Rural Affairs,
1856

AN ITALIAN COTTAGE

FIRST FLOOR
PLAN

For a smaller sized country or farm house, combining something of the characteristics of the tasteful cottagewith a convenient home arrangement, we furnish this design.

With the exception, perhaps, of the arched veranda, there is no exterior ornament whatever. It will be observed that the roof is steeper than in Italian houses generally, giving more room in the chamber apartments, and preventing danger of leakage. This steepness can be only adopted in one-and-a-half story houses as it would impart too heavy an appearance to any other.

There are three principal rooms below, besides a small bedroom, and there may be four above, one each over the parlor and kitchen and two over the nursery.

This plan possesses some important advantages, among which we may mention the convenience of a hall extending through the house, without occupying much space, from which every room on the ground floor is entered. The chimneys being near the centre, but little heat is lost through the outside walls. The kitchen has four closets, (marked c,) and the nursery one.

In such cases as do not require a nursery, the parlor may be changed to a dining and living room, and the present nursery transformed into a neat and comfortable parlor.

A SOUTHERN COUNTRY HOUSE

Fruitlands Cottage,
Augusta, Georgia

Daniel H. Jacques,
*The House: A Manual of
Rural Architecture*,
1866

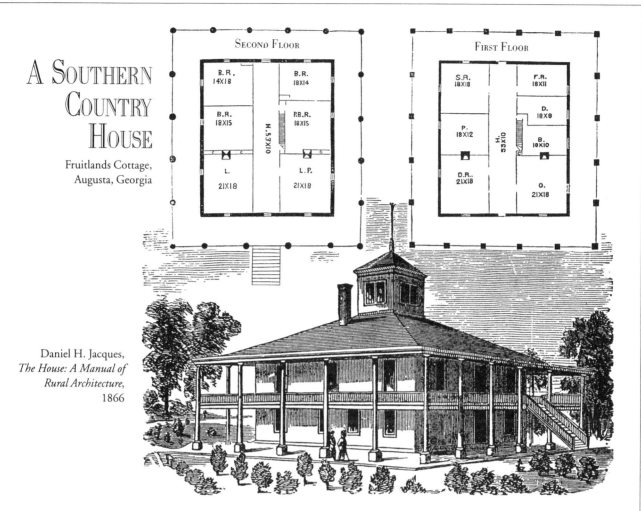

The most obvious requirements of a Southern country house are: ample space, shade, and ventilation. Where land is abundant and cheap, the ground plan should be so extended as to get all the room needed as near the ground as possible and avoid the fatiguing ascent of high flights of stairs. On any proper location, where the land is high, dry, and airy, a basement entirely above the surface, with one story above that, for parlor, sleeping rooms, etc., will be found well adapted to the wants of a modern family.

Externally, the house should present a reasonable degree of architectural style corresponding with the interior, and in harmony with the surrounding scenery. Thus, while a Swiss or Gothic cottage would be out of place in a low, level, and warm country, a flat-roofed Tuscan or Italian villa would be equally inappropriate amid the heavy snow storms and wild tempests of the Alps. This sense of fitness should naturally lead us, in the erection of a country house for the South to study carefully the peculiarities of our climate and surroundings, in addition to our own individual wants, and to modify existing modes into what some one has called the "comfortable and convenient," as distinguished from the merely ornamental styles of architecture. —D. Redmond, *The Southern Cultivator*, 1866

First Floor Plan: H., hall, 53x10 feet; D.R., dining room, 21x18; P., pantry, 18x12, adjoining the dining room; S.R., store room, 18x18, next to pantry; O., office; B., bathroom; D., dairy, 18x9; F.R., fruit room.

Second Floor Plan: H., hall, 53x10 feet; L., library, 21x18; B.R., three bedrooms respectively 18x15, 18x14, and 18x11; P., parlor, 21x18; P.B.R., parlor bedroom, 18x15; c., closets.

A Small, Complete Dwelling

B.W. Steere, Adrian, Michigan, *The Register of Rural Affairs*, 1873
(Barn and Background, 1871)

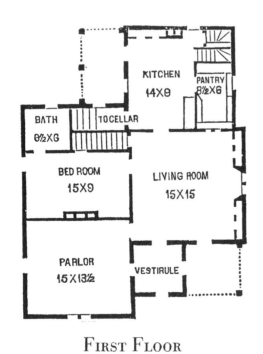

FIRST FLOOR

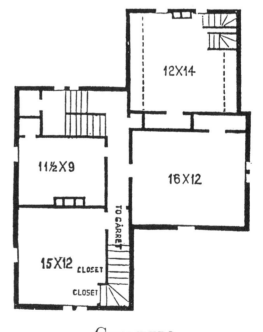

CHAMBERS

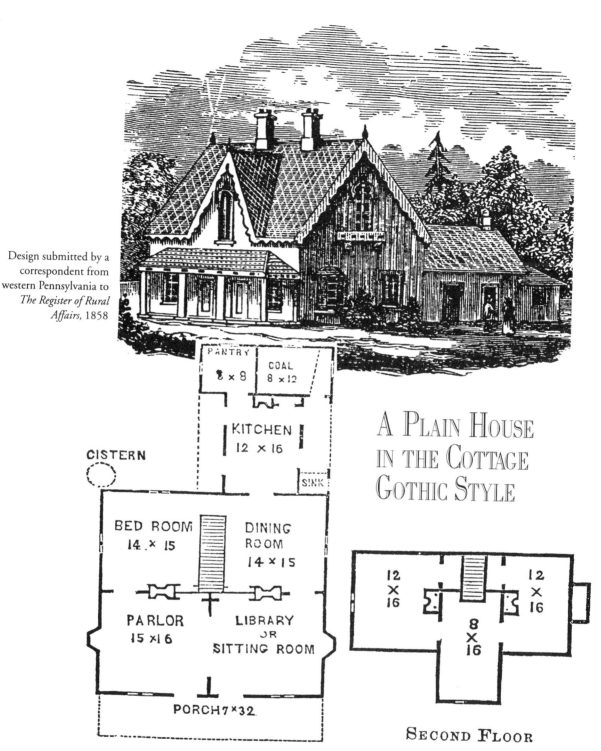

Design submitted by a correspondent from western Pennsylvania to *The Register of Rural Affairs*, 1858

PANTRY 8 × 8

COAL 8 × 12

KITCHEN 12 × 16

CISTERN

SINK

A Plain House
in the Cottage
Gothic Style

BED ROOM 14 × 15

DINING ROOM 14 × 15

PARLOR 15 × 16

LIBRARY or SITTING ROOM

PORCH 7 × 32

First Floor

12 × 16

12 × 16

8 × 16

Second Floor

Farmers mixed styles freely in their homes. The Gothic roof and carved wood trim on the front of this house distract the eye from a very plain kitchen ell. The columns and trim on the front porch are Grecian. The plan, with its two front doors, is an echo of the traditional hall and parlor house that the designer must have seen back east.

Most architects of the day would be appalled at this house. They often boasted that their own designs were "simple," which seems odd from today's view. To them, the term meant that the design had the benefit of a consistent style throughout.

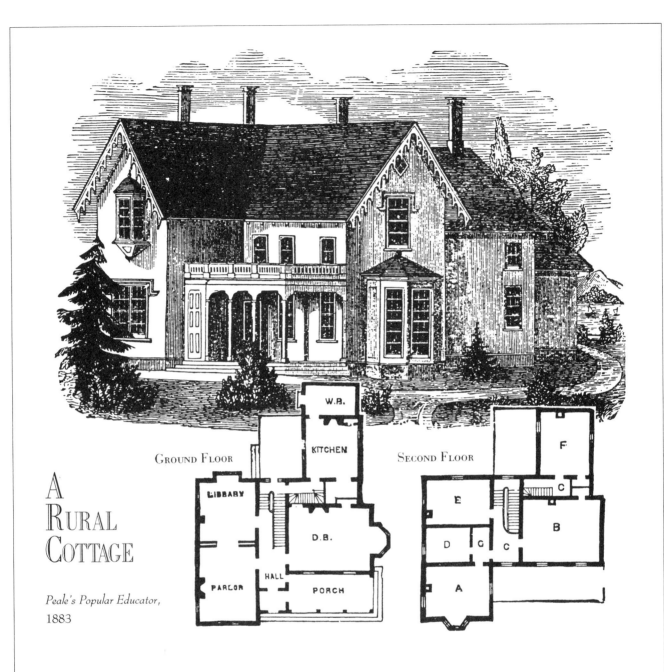

A
RURAL
COTTAGE

Peale's Popular Educator,
1883

The accompanying plan of a rural cottage was awarded a premium which was offered some few years ago. The outside appearance is attractive, light and pleasant, and is not overly ornamental, a great fault with many modern houses. The rooms are large and most conveniently arranged, every room of the ground floor being pleasant enough for a parlor or a living room.

Ground Floor: D.R., dining room, 18 feet 9 inches by 15 feet; Parlor 18 feet 9 inches by 14 feet 6 inches; F, servants' bedroom, 12 feet 6 inches by 14 feet 6 inches; Library, 15 feet by 14 feet 6 inches; Kitchen, 12 feet 6 inches by 13 feet 6 inches; W.R., wash room, 12 feet by 8 feet; Hall, 6 feet 5 inches in width.

Second Floor: A, bedroom, 14 feet 5 inches by 11 feet 9 inches; B, chamber, 18 feet 9 inches by 15 feet; C, C, halls; D, bedroom, 9 feet 6 inches by 11 feet; E, bedroom, 14 feet 6 inches by 11 feet; F, servants' bedroom, 14 feet 6 inches by 14 feet 6 inches; G, passage, 3 feet 6 inches in width.

A Compact Square Dwelling

W.B. Steere, of Adrian, Michigan,
The Register of Rural Affairs,
1873

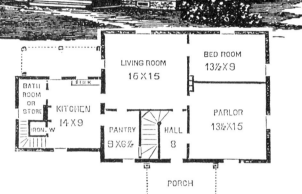

The ground plan of this design is so nearly square that those who prefer the four-sided or square roof can adopt it.

I must confess however to a strong objection to such a roof on a house fairly in the country. It seems to look well enough in town or suburb, but the upper horizontal line of the span roof, with its handsome gables, will generally afford the beholder most pleasure, and appears to harmonize best with country scenery. There is also a practical reason for it worth considering. The good housewife prizes a fine, open garret for many purposes. Not the least of these is having a place for drying clothes in cold or stormy weather, where they can hang regardless of thieves or sudden rain, until she is ready to iron them. This is a principal reason why at least one wing of some of the other designs is carried up two stories when good proportion in so narrow a building seems to require less height. The roofs also are pretty steep, allowing snow and rain to slip off easily, making the roof more durable, beside giving better head room.

This is also rather in violation of what is usually taught in architectural works, for there we are apt to find the flattest roofs on two-story houses. The idea appears to be that the house with steep roof, being actually higher, must necessarily appear so. This I believe to be a mistake, at least on rather narrow buildings. Having given particular attention to the subject for some time past, and made many comparisons, it is found that houses with flattish roofs invariably look higher than their steeper roofed neighbors. It would appear that we judge mainly by apparent height

PRINCIPAL FLOOR

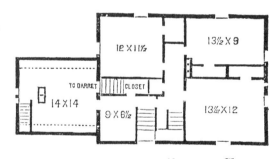

SECOND FLOOR

of the sides, or distance from side eaves to the ground. Now the steep roof, with modern or wide projection, shuts down over the sides and, as it were, covers up or absorbs a portion of this side height into itself, and we lose sight of it in the impression made upon the mind.

Whether this can be adopted as a principle or not, it is a great pity for the good of the roof and all beneath it, that some noted authority has not long ago laid down the rule that no shingle roof shall have less than 30 degrees or one-third pitch.

A Bracketed Farmhouse of Wood, A.J. Downing, Architect, *The Architecture of Country Houses*, 1850 This also appeared as "A Country House" in the March 1850 issue of *The Horticulturist*

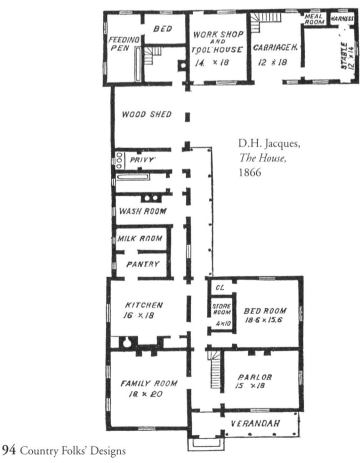

D.H. Jacques, *The House*, 1866

The farmhouse on page 95 shows a resemblance to A.J. Downing's earlier "Bracketed Farmhouse of Wood," but that wasn't the intention. When farmer Lewis Allen designed it, he had no desire to make it as fashionable as it appears. Throughout his book *Rural Architecture,* he complained that the architects that he hired to prepare the drawings took liberties with his ideas. On this engraving he noted "the main roof of the house is made to appear like a double, or gambrel, roof, breaking at the intersection of the gable, or hanging roof over the ends. This is not so intended." Historian Sally McMurray found that Allen built the original of this design, in Grand Island, New York, with a simple gable roof.

The plan at left is an 1866 adaptation of Allen's by New York architect John Crumly.

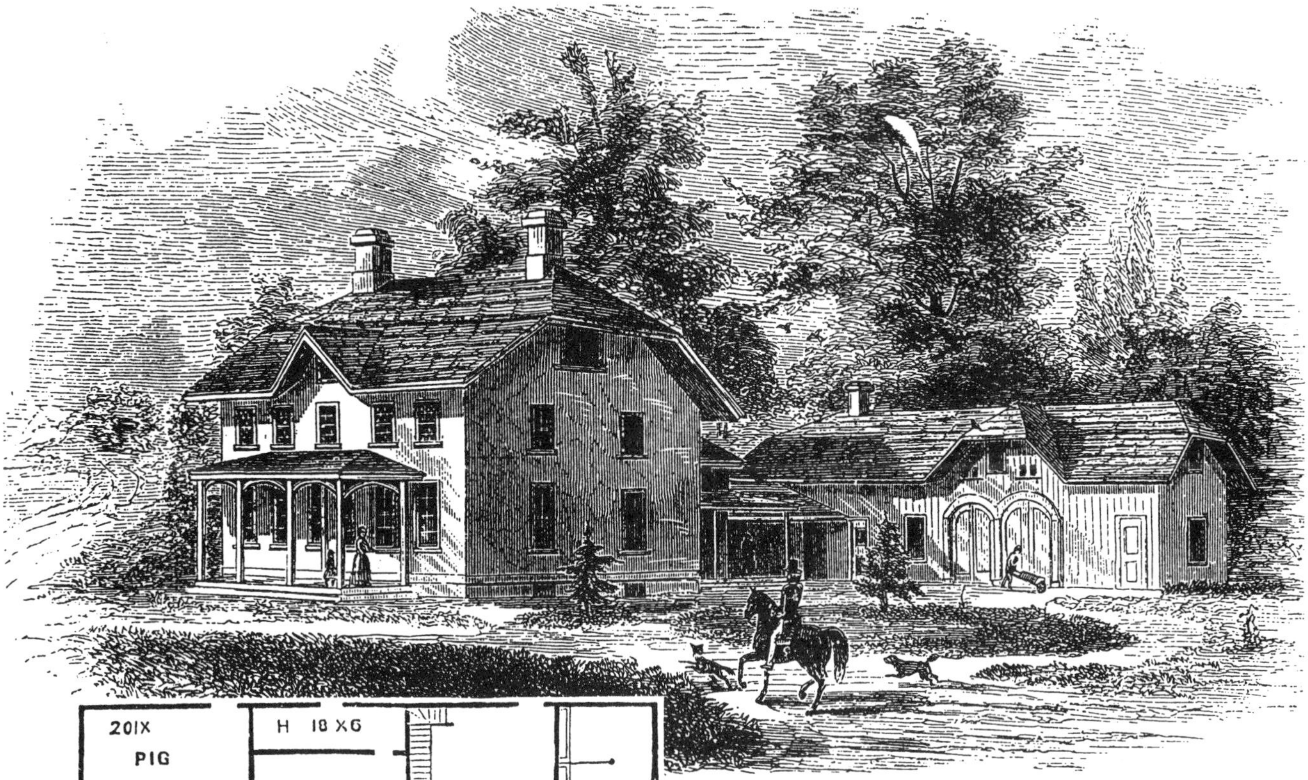

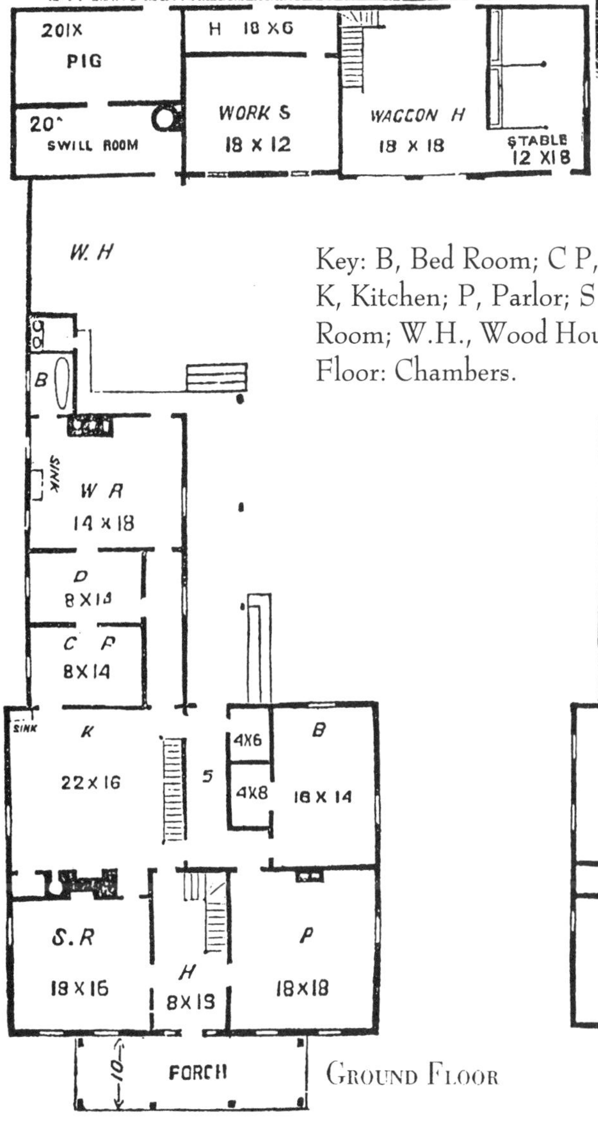
20IX
PIG
20^
SWILL ROOM
H 18 X6
WORK S
18 X 12
WAGGON H
18 X 18
STABLE
12 X18
W. H
B
SINK
W R
14 x 18
D
8X14
C P
8X14
SINK
K
22X16
5
4X6
4X8
B
16 X 14
S.R
18 X16
H
8X13
P
18X18
10
PORCH

Ground Floor

Key: B, Bed Room; C P, Closet and Pantry: D, Dairy or Milk Room; H, Hall; K, Kitchen; P, Parlor; S R, Sitting Room; W R, Wash Room with B, Bathing Room; W.H., Wood House; Work S, Work Shed with H, Hen House. Second Floor: Chambers.

A Farmhouse

Lewis F. Allen, *Rural Architecture*, 1852

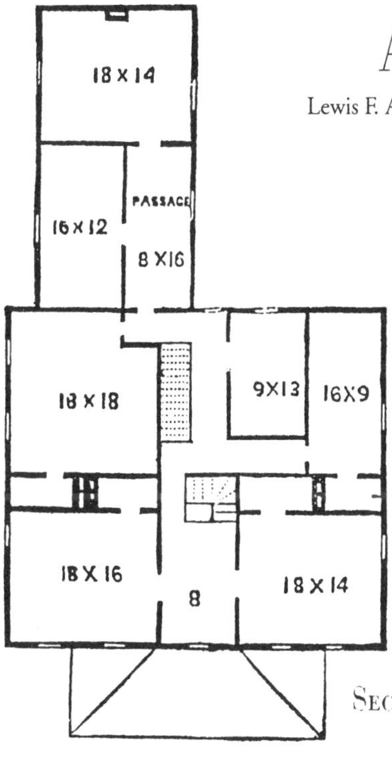
18 X 14
16 X 12
PASSAGE
8 X16
18 X 18
9X13
16X9
18X16
8
18 X 14

Second Floor

A Farm House for a Small Family

The Register of Rural Affairs, 1861

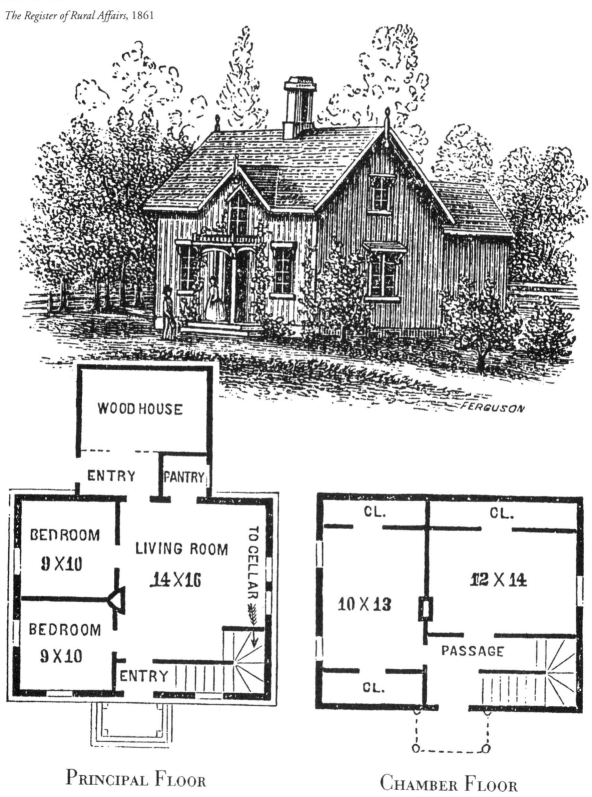

FERGUSON

WOOD HOUSE

ENTRY   PANTRY

BEDROOM
9 X 10

LIVING ROOM
14 X 16

TO CELLAR

BEDROOM
9 X 10

ENTRY

CL.   CL.

10 X 13   12 X 14

PASSAGE

CL.

PRINCIPAL FLOOR   CHAMBER FLOOR

A Dwelling with Wings

B.W. Steere, Adrian, Michigan, *The Register of Rural Affairs*, 1873

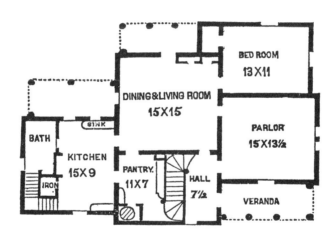

FIRST FLOOR PLAN

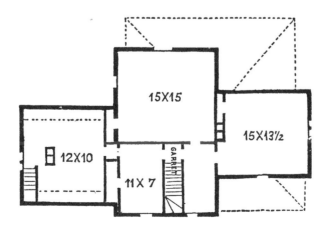

SECOND FLOOR PLAN

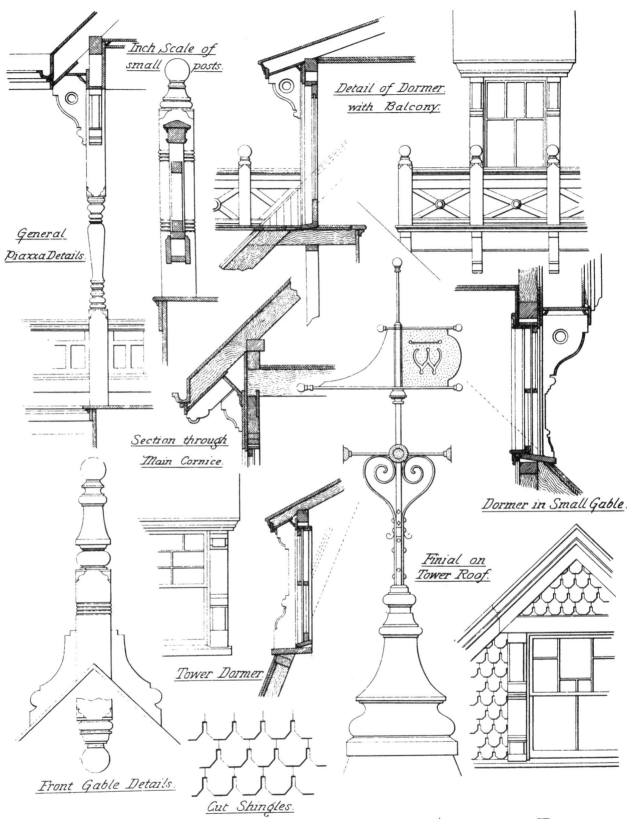

Inch Scale of small posts.

Detail of Dormer with Balcony.

General Piazza Details.

Section through Main Cornice.

Dormer in Small Gable.

Finial on Tower Roof.

Tower Dormer.

Front Gable Details.

Cut Shingles.

EXTERIOR DETAILS

Howe & Dodd, Architects,
*Comstock's Modern Architectural
Designs and Details,* 1881

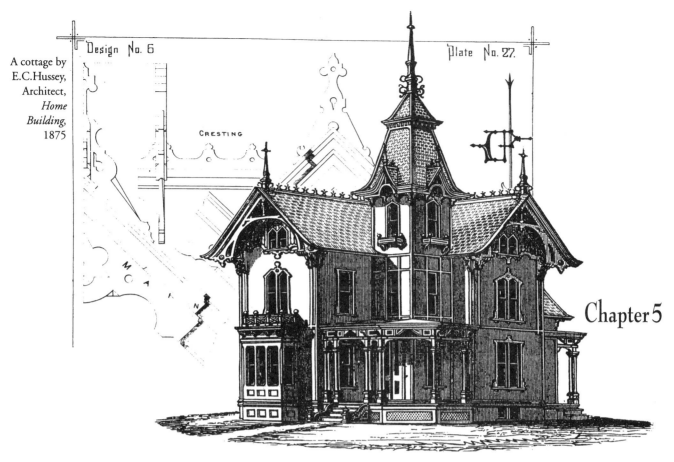

Design No. 6

CRESTING

Plate No. 27.

A cottage by
E.C. Hussey,
Architect,
*Home
Building,*
1875

Chapter 5

Building Details

One thing that high-style urban architects and country builders shared was an enthusiasm for decorative details. Architects filled their plan books with drawings of carved and turned wood ornaments. Farmers decorated their porches with the same. They bought fancy panel doors and pretty round top windows. They built big, elaborate ventilators for their barns that rivaled church spires in their fine workmanship.

There was, however a limit to how they'd use the high-style gewgawgery. Architects liked gable top finials, flying verge boards and cresting that ran the length of a roof ridge. These were all exposed to the worst of the weather and required constant repair. Farmers seemed to prefer ornaments that nestled under protecting roofs. Brackets on the underside of roof overhangs were very popular; so were fancy posts and braces under porch roofs.

Architects catered to country builders' desire for details. First their books provided drawings of the ornaments of specific house designs. Gradually, they started selling books full of generic woodwork details, often without the homes to hang them on. This suited farmers just fine. Their concept of decoration was a bit different than the high-style standard. Architects used exterior decoration to accent a particular building style. Gothic houses got board and batten siding and pointy carvings that accented that style,s verticality; Italian or Tuscan buildings had heavy roof brackets and rounded accents that complemented their horizontal spread; Greek or Roman Revival houses would have classic columns and smooth moldings that mimicked the stone work of ancient temples. A farmer's place might have a little bit of all.

It is hard to justify the farmers' love of gingerbread. Everything else they built was so practical. There may be some practical aspects to their use of ornament: columns or a fancy portico would help strangers find the best door to use; and barn cupolas certainly attracted distant travelers who might be looking for lodging.

Historian Thomas Hubka has shown how some Maine farmers spread the visual effect of a new house across the old farmstead by decorating their barns to match. Farms were commercial establishments. Today, stores constantly update their appearance to catch customer's attention. It may have been something like that. Or, it could just have been whimsy like whirligigs and crazy quilts. Country folk liked those too.

VERANDAS & PORCHES

George E. Woodward, Architect, *Woodward's National Architect*, 1868

SECTION AT P.

SECTION AT R.

BALUSTER.

SECTION AT A.

CAPITAL AT C.

EXAMPLES OF BRACKETS

George E. Woodward, Architect, *Woodward's National Architect*, 1868

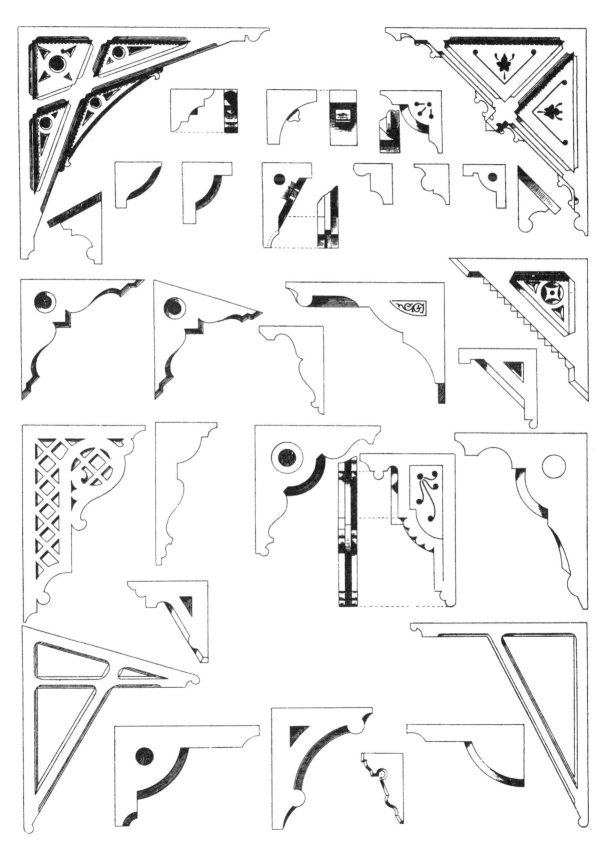

Piazzas

Comstock's Modern Architectural Designs and Details, 1881

WOODEN CORNICES

ELEVATION. SECTION. ELEVATION SECTION.

BRACKET BRACKET.

RAFTERS and SCROLLS.

RAILINGS

TURNED WORK

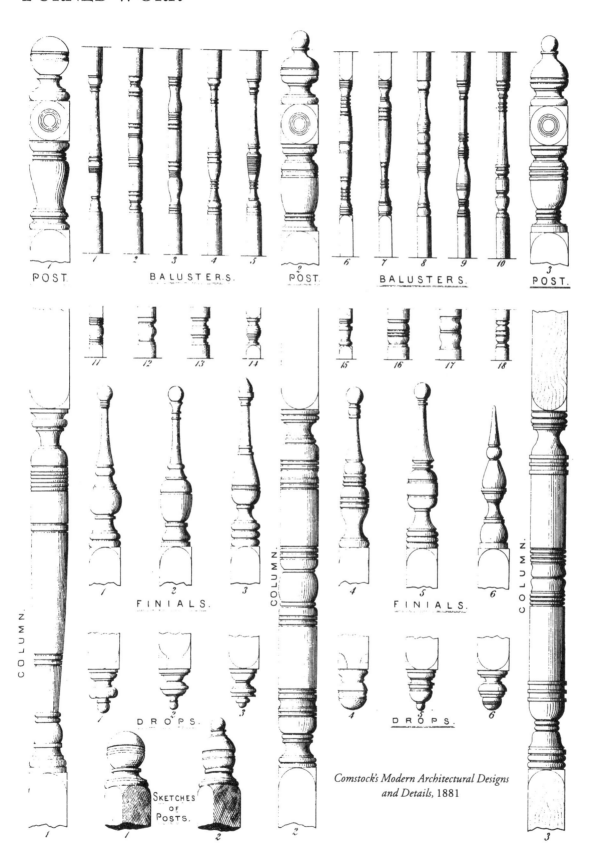

POST.   BALUSTERS.   POST.   BALUSTERS.   POST.

COLUMN.   FINIALS.   COLUMN.   FINIALS.   COLUMN.

DROPS.   DROPS.

SKETCHES OF POSTS.

Comstock's Modern Architectural Designs and Details, 1881

VARIOUS DETAILS

George E. Woodward, Architect, *Woodward's National Architect,* 1868

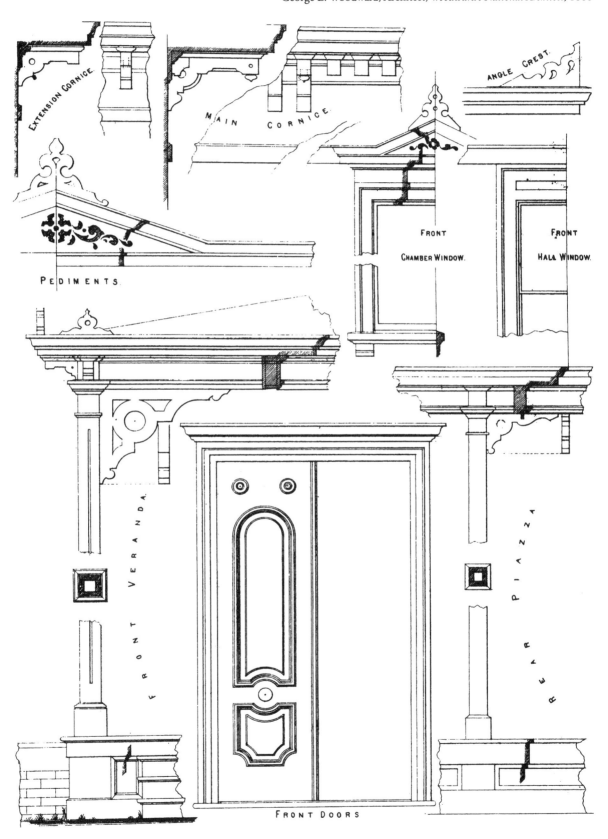

OUTBUILDING DETAILS

George E. Harney, Architect, *Bicknell's Wooden and Brick Buildings with Details*, 1875

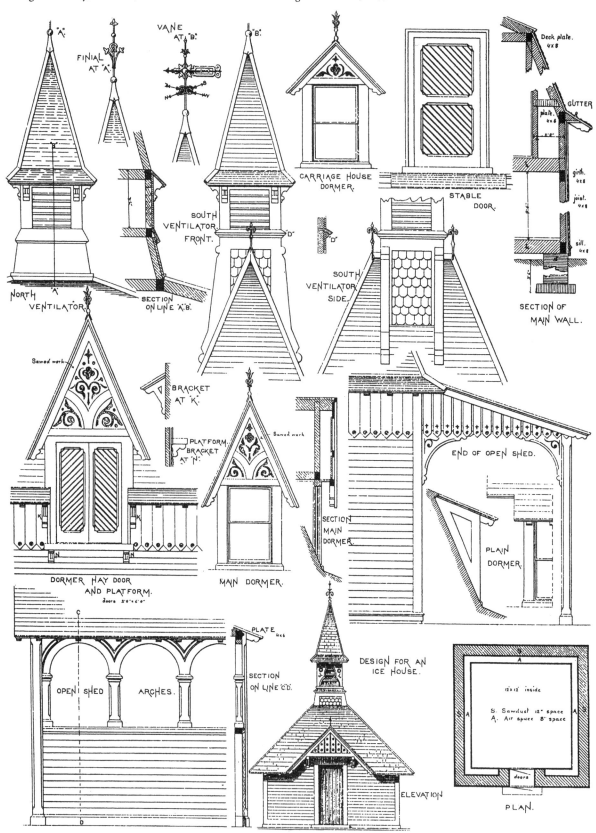

VANE AT "B".

FINIAL AT "A".

"A".

"B".

NORTH VENTILATOR.

SOUTH VENTILATOR FRONT.

SECTION ON LINE "A".B".

SOUTH VENTILATOR SIDE.

CARRIAGE HOUSE DORMER.

STABLE DOOR.

Deck plate. 4x8

GUTTER

plate. 4x8

girth. 4x8

joist. 4x8

sill. 4x8

SECTION OF MAIN WALL.

Sawed work.

BRACKET AT "K".

PLATFORM BRACKET AT "N".

Sawed work.

SECTION MAIN DORMER.

END OF OPEN SHED.

PLAIN DORMER.

DORMER HAY DOOR AND PLATFORM.
doors 2'-0"×6'-0"

MAIN DORMER.

OPEN SHED ARCHES.

PLATE 4x6

SECTION ON LINE "C".D".

DESIGN FOR AN ICE HOUSE.

ELEVATION

12'×12' inside

S. Sawdust 12" space
A. Air space 8" space

doors

PLAN.

Chapter 6

Barns, Carriage Houses & Outbuildings

Does this barn look familiar? If you drive country roads from Maine to Texas, from the Dakotas to the Carolinas, you'll see it. It might be red, white or weathered gray. It's roof could be slate, wood shingles or just strips of tar paper. It might sit alone, on the side of the road, or it might be quilted into a patchwork of barns and sheds. There is one in western Connecticut that's weed-covered and so rundown that it can barely hold up its rusted roof. There's another in a Wisconsin farmer's 1880 painting that's forever new with bright yellow paint.

You can always recognize this barn. The big doors are right in the center and open on the third level. The roof is steep, 12 inches up for every 12 over. Yesterday's builders called that a "square" pitch. If it isn't set into the side of a hill, there is a earth ramp to the doors.

It's a great design: simple, pretty and efficient. This barn is big enough for a small farm and small enough to be a second barn or field barn on a larger place. The lowest level is a cellar for root storage and for stock. The hill and the masonry walls give shelter from winter winds and keep it cool in summer. The next floor is for more animals. The third level is a work space with storage for grain and tools. Hay and grain, stored in a loft above that, will stay dry and act as a blanket of insulation. It all makes for easier work. Grain, hay or straw are just dropped down to the threshing floor or animal stalls as needed.

The design was first published in April, 1870, in *The American Agriculturist,* a farm journal that had subscribers throughout the U.S. and Canada and had both English and German editions. It was hardly revolutionary. It borrowed on earlier traditions; it was just a three bay, New England, English barn built on top of a Pennsylvania German stone cellar. But, it also presented two innovations. It suggested that farmers in flat country build a earth berm to the upper levels, and it had a timber frame that was open enough to allow the use of a hay fork for lifting grain to the loft.

It was common for a prosperous farm family to have one or two barns and 10 or more outbuildings on their farmstead. Every home needed a carriage house, a stable and a woodshed. Progressive farmers needed special buildings for the various processes of their trade. Smokehouses, tool-sheds, dairy houses, icehouses, corn-cribs and cobble shops were common. Even in country villages, most families kept chickens, pigs and a cow and grew fruit and vegetables, so even village lots had their share of farm buildings. A few architects included barns and outbuildings in their plan books, but most just ignored them. Farmers filled the void by filling their journals and plan books with designs.

Barns and outbuildings were symbols of a farm family's success. The specialty buildings showed industry and the diversity of their output. A big barn bragged of efficient farming and abundant harvests; poor farmers, with little to store, didn't need one. It advertized good produce and clean lodging to passersby. Architect A.J. Downing thought that a barn needed "unobtrusive tone of color," but farmers thought differently and painted them bright.

A Cheap Stable for Two Horses

George E. Harney, Architect, *Barns, Outbuildings and Fences*, 1870

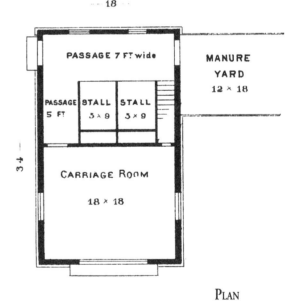

Plan

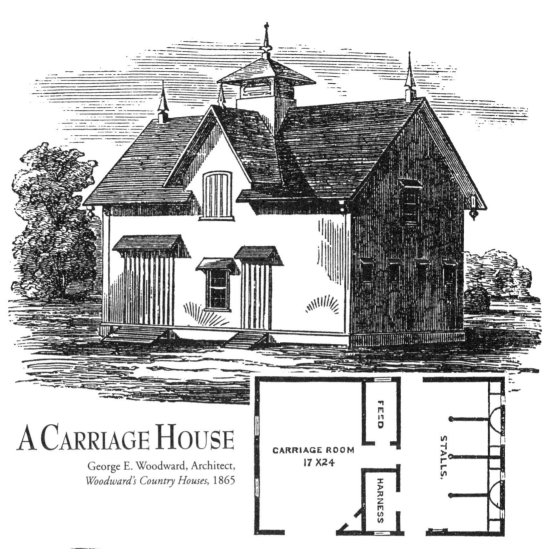

A CARRIAGE HOUSE

George E. Woodward, Architect,
Woodward's Country Houses, 1865

CARRIAGE ROOM
17 X 24

FEED

HARNESS

STALLS.

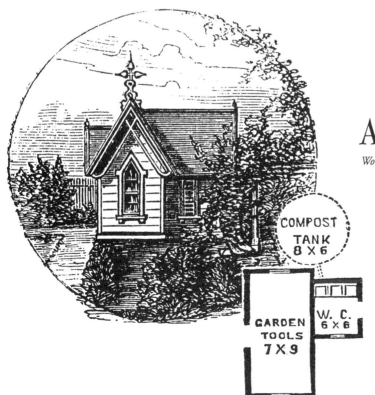

A TOOL-HOUSE, ETC.

Woodward's Cottages and Farm Houses, 1867

COMPOST
TANK
8 X 6

W. C.
6 X 6

GARDEN
TOOLS
7 X 9

A Cheap Stable for Two Horses and a Cow

This design was built a few years ago for a gentleman in Massachusetts, at a cost of less than five hundred dollars, and is a fair sample of the accommodation usually required for an ordinary New England village stable.

The second floor is for storing hay, which is supplied to the troughs by means of shoots. A large ventilating shaft terminates in the ventilator, seen in the perspective view. The manure-yard is on the right, and is enclosed by a high fence, so overrun by Virginia creeper that it is hardly seen. And here let us remark, that every stable, however small or however situated, but particularly if it be on a village lot, should have its manure-yard always enclosed by a fence or screen of some kind. A manure heap is never a pretty thing to look at, but a screen can always be made attractive, especially if covered with vines or cloaked by evergreens. —George E. Harney, Architect, *Barns, Outbuildings and Fences*, 1870

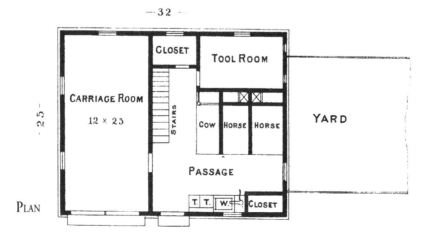

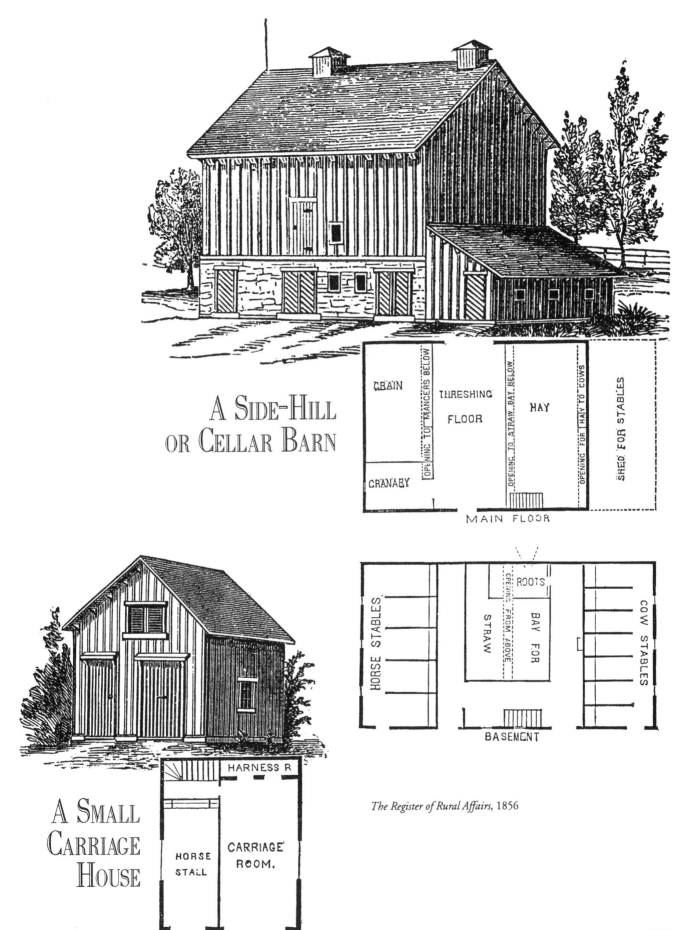

A SIDE-HILL
OR CELLAR BARN

GRAIN THRESHING FLOOR HAY SHED FOR STABLES
OPENING TO MANGERS BELOW
GRANARY
OPENING TO STRAW BAY BELOW
OPENING FOR HAY TO COWS
MAIN FLOOR

HORSE STABLES
ROOTS
STRAW BAY FOR
OPENING FROM ABOVE
COW STABLES
BASEMENT

The Register of Rural Affairs, 1856

A SMALL
CARRIAGE
HOUSE

HARNESS R
HORSE STALL
CARRIAGE ROOM.

Farm Barn and Hennery

The illustration on the opposite page gives a correct idea of a country farm barn, which will interest those who are agriculturally inclined. To the farmer it is one of the most important things how he shall house his stock, and provide storage for his grain, fodder, etc., and yet do it in an economical manner; and the many farm barns that are to be seen, with their chopped up and checkered appearance, indicate that this matter has not had a proper amount of study and forethought. The farmer goes on and builds a little at a time, never thinking or looking far enough ahead to know what his wants really may be when his farm is being worked to its proper capacity. If you own a farm, and intend to be a good farmer, start out with a determination to have only suitable farm buildings, such as will look well from your neighbor's house. Let your barns look like barns, your houses like houses. We would not for anything have your barns be mistaken for houses, or your houses for barns; for such things we have seen, and it makes us feel as if there was a screw loose somewhere. Barns should not be built for show.

They should, of course, be made to look well, and be pleasant spots in the landscape, and built in the most substantial manner possible. They should be arranged to save as much labor as possible in the care of the animals that are to be housed and fed in them. Let them be well ventilated and lighted, properly floored; the stone work of the foundation thoroughly built, not dry, but laid up in good cement mortar. Don't invite the rats, as they will come without. The Hennery here shown was carried out as an addition to barn at Hill-side farm, New Milford, Conn., owned by Egbert Marsh, Esq., and shows Mr. Marsh's ideas of what a well regulated Hennery should be to make it both a pleasure and a profit. As the shed below is a necessity in connection with barn, and a roof indispensable, the only additional expense is the floor, one side and ends, with the interior fittings, to make a Hennery which will accommodate easily one hundred to two hundred. The run from the Hennery is so arranged that fowls can be let into the shed or directly out of doors. —George and Charles Palliser, Architects, *Palliser's Model Homes*, 1878

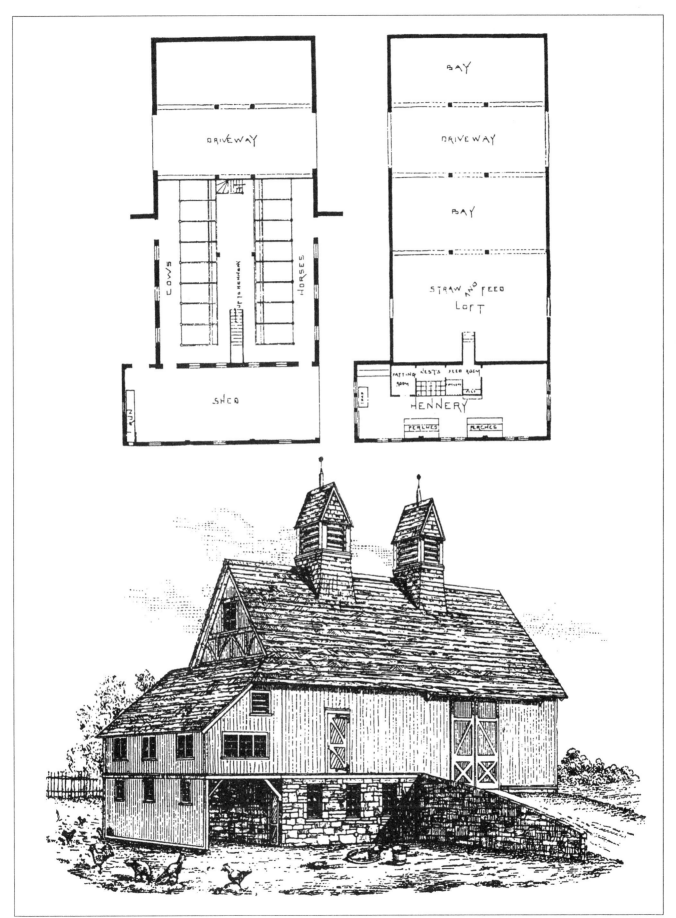

BAY

DRIVEWAY

DRIVEWAY

BAY

COWS

HORSES

UP TO MOWSTOW

STRAW AND FEED LOFT

SHED

RUN

FATTING ROOM

NESTS

FEED ROOM

TRAP

ROOST

HENNERY

PERCHES

PERCHES

A WOODEN STABLE FOR THREE HORSES

This stable is built of wood in the simplest manner, and covered with vertical boards and battens. The roof is hipped and covered with sawed shingles. Each stall has a ventilator near the ceiling, and there is a shaft two and a half feet square running from the ceiling to the ventilator in the roof, communicating also with the ceiling over the cow stall. The large doors are made to slide on the inside. The inside partitions are of tongued and grooved pine boards, and the floors and stall divisions are of two-inch plank. The heelposts at the stalls are turned out of hard wood, and firmly secured to the floor joists. —George E. Harney, Architect, *Barns, Outbuildings and Fences,* 1870

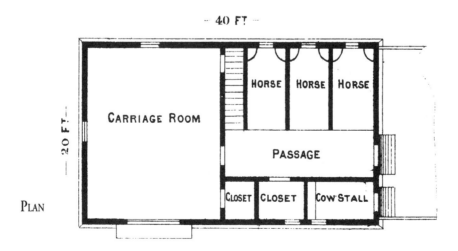

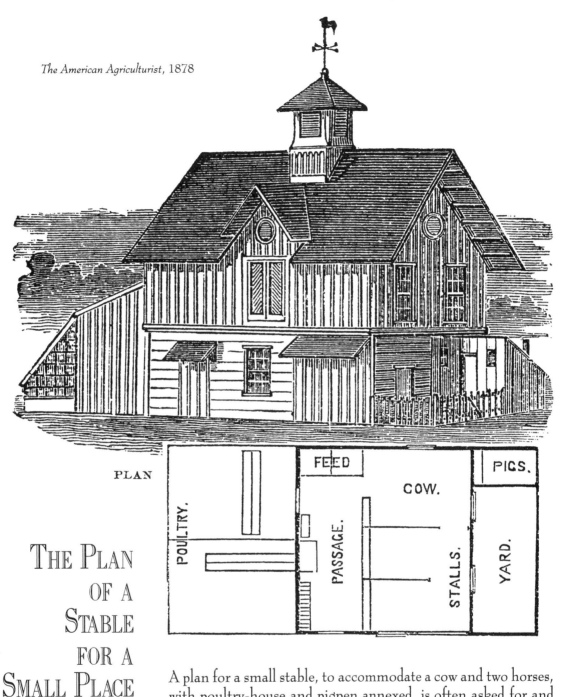

The American Agriculturist, 1878

PLAN

POULTRY.

FEED

COW.

PASSAGE.

STALLS.

PIGS.

YARD.

The Plan of a Stable for a Small Place

A plan for a small stable, to accommodate a cow and two horses, with poultry-house and pigpen annexed, is often asked for and we give one. The ground plan is 34 feet long, and 18 feet wide. The central part comprises two horse stalls, 5x10 feet, and a loose box for a cow, 7.5x10 feet, with a passage, in which is a feed bin, room for a fodder cutter and feed box, and stairs to the hay loft above. The poultry house adjoins the passage from which two doors open into it. This house is 18x12 feet, and has a sloping front of glazed sash.

A SMALL OHIO BARN

Illustration from Byron D. Halstead's , *Barn Plans and Outbuildings*, 1881

LOFT PLAN

FLOOR PLAN

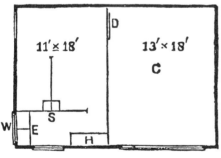

T.H.R.,Jr. of Dayton, Ohio, having seen the "Plan for a Small Barn" in our September issue, sends a plan of his barn which he has recently built. He thinks it preferable for a small place to the other one, "as it will cost less, being smaller and yet sufficiently roomy for two horses, or a horse and a cow and two vehicles, besides presenting a better appearance. It also obviates the necessity of going behind the horses when feeding, which is often desirable, as in families having no hired help the feeding is sometimes entrusted to the children." The outside appearance is shown and is certainly pleasing to the eye. The ground floor is 18 by 24 feet, 8 feet between joists. The carriage room, C, is 13 by 18 feet, with sliding doors 10 feet wide. The horse is led through the door D, from the carriage room to the stable. The box E, containing food, connects by two spouts with grain bins in the loft. The hay shoot is shown at S, and is between the mangers. The harness closet, H, is placed under the stairway. A window, W, gives light to the feed room and the stalls. The loft is 6.5 feet to the plates, and with a three-quarter pitch to the roof there is ample room for hay and straw. The barn is built of hemlock, sided with 7/8 inch dressed boards, 12 inches wide, and battened. It cost complete and painted, $200: —*The American Agriculturist*, 1880

A Basement Barn

George E. Harney, Architect,
Barns, Outbuildings and Fences, 1870

We here present a design for a barn which, though not in reality a side-hill barn, combines all the advantages of that manner of building, with more perfect light, more thorough ventilation, and more extent of yard room; in fact, the basement is a full story entirely above the ground on the two longest sides, and having windows and doors opening out upon two barn-yards, one on the north and one on the south.

The foundation and basement are of rubble stone, laid in cement. The superstructure is of frame, boarded and battened, and the roof is slated. The eaves project some three feet, and are carried on heavy brackets, and the ridge of the roof is surmounted by a ventilator. The doors are all made in two halves, so that the upper half may be open for air while the lower half is shut. The inclined planes at each end which lead to the main floors, have sides of masonry filled in with stones and gravel, and under one of them is a large root cellar, opening into the wagon shed, on the left of the plan.

The perspective view is taken from the north side. The winter barn-yard and the entrances to the basement, are on the opposite or south side, as will be seen by the plan.

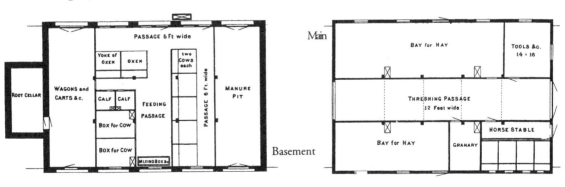

New York architect George Harney presented an interesting blend of tradition and innovation in his design for this barn. The stone basement is similar to basements on traditional Pennsylvania German side-hill barns. Here, on a flat site, gravel ramps give access to the main floor. The wooden barn above it is a common New England barn. The doors, "made in two halves" are Dutch. The Italianate cupola is decorative whimsy: only the small louvered panels function as ventilators and they could have been built much more simply.

DESIGN
FOR A
POULTRY
HOUSE

George E. Harney,
Architect,
*Barns, Outbuildings and
Fences*, 1870

SOUTH

YARD   ONE ACRE

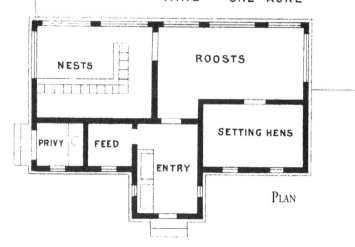

NESTS   ROOSTS

PRIVY   FEED   SETTING HENS

ENTRY

PLAN

Chapter 7

Farmstead Plans & the Country Landscape

By the early 19th century, most of the settled areas of America had been stripped of their native trees. Wood burning for heat and the new steam-powered industries, lumber for the rural building boom and the constant clearing of new farm fields left a barren landscape. Our vast eastern forests were reduced to less than a fifth of their original size. Without the binding roots, topsoil washed into rivers. Without trees to break it, wind ripped at walls and fences.

Country folk started to appreciate the damage they had done. They knew that homes shaded by trees were cooler in summer. Farmers learned that their livestock fared better in tree-shaded fields. They found that thickets of pines kept them and their stock protected from winter winds. They started replanting the countryside at the same time that they were replanning their homes and farms.

New farmsteads were arranged on a rigid grid plan. The walls and ridges of all buildings were usually parallel to the road and almost always square with each other. If a neighbor's place was nearby, buildings would be neighborly. Adjacent farmsteads, just like country village homes, usually had the same orientation and

the same distance of setback from the road. The buildings were arranged around a central yard or along a common drive. The building grid allowed efficient work and an orderly way of adding new buildings or expanding old ones.

Progressive farmers rotated their crops to preserve their soil. They constantly experimented with new crops and new breeds of livestock. Their buildings had to change often to their new methods of production and storage. The yard and grid plan was perfect. New buildings facing on the yard were convenient to the old ones. No new access drives were needed. Building on the square meant that new structures could easily nestle against or between old ones. Walls, foundations and cisterns were shared, reducing building costs.

The new farmstead had such an advantage in efficiency and flexibility that older places were renovated to a similar plan. In winter, a farm family would invite their neighbors to a "moving bee" and hitch all of the neighborhood's oxen to a house or barn. They'd drag the building over the frozen ground into a new position on the farmyard grid. With new siding or a fresh coat of paint, the old building would take on a new life.

At first, all planting followed the same rigid geometry. Shade trees lined drives and followed fences; fruit trees were arranged in neat rows. Decorative plants and flowers were given a small rectangular plot before the front door. This dooryard was usually fenced to protect it from stray stock. Early farm views even show dooryard flowers in straight rows. But, the same urban designers who introduced the new building styles also presented a new style in planting that country folk found both attractive and practical.

The new style was called "picturesque," "natural," or, like every new style, "modern." It tried to match the wondrous variety of the natural landscape. It originated on country estates in England but was introduced here in Andrew Jackson Downing's 1841 book, *A Treatise on the Theory and Practice of Landscape Gardening, Adapted to North America: with a View to the Improvement of Country Residences*. Despite that title, the tome was artfully written and beautifully illustrated. Downing, a nurseryman before becoming a high-style designer, presented native trees as if they were rare ornamentals, showing how each could be best used in decorative planting.

For country folk, the style was perfect. Weed saplings could be transformed, by simple transplanting, into elegant decorations. The old geometric style was incredibly inefficient. One tree uprooted by a storm would ruin a procession. Rows of all-the-same trees died together with blights. With the modern method, a pretty thicket could be both ornament and wood-lot. Where old trees were culled for firewood or lumber, seedlings grew in their place and added to the variegation. Shade trees and pine windbreaks could be planted just where they were needed without concern for symmetry.

It didn't seem to occur to anyone at the time, but the natural style of landscaping was the perfect balance for the new stern geometry of country buildings. Orderly clusters of simple farm structures against the wild green of nature or natural-looking plantings are still visually stunning.

AN OLD FARMSTEAD

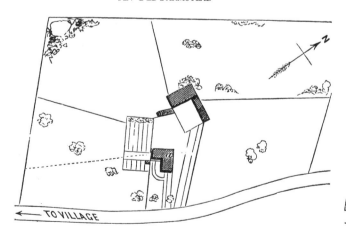

THE SAME PLACE RENOVATED

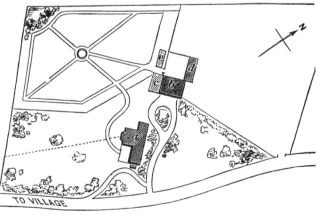

These plans of a small Connecticut farm are from Donald Mitchell's 1867 book, *Rural Studies*. In the renovated plan, the naturalistic landscaping contrasts with the straight, square alignment of the home and its outbuildings. The house, marked "a," is the same one in each plan. For the renovation it was moved and enlarged. The dotted lines show the sight line to the view of the village shown in the oval above.

A Comfortable Country Residence

The plan represents a comfortable farm residence, where the owner wishes to have everything neat and in good taste, but cannot expend much in ornamental gardening. The grounds are laid out in as simple a manner as practicable, so as to accord with good taste. As represented in the plan, they comprise from two to three acres, including the lawn, half of the fruit garden, and most of the kitchen garden. The dwelling is approached by a good and well made gravel road, and the surrounding grounds are planted with handsome shade trees; those towards the rear may be the hardier, more vigorous and symmetrical fruit trees, such as will flourish in grass as for example, the Buffum, Boussock and Howell pears, and the Elton, Rockport and Black Tartarian cherries. The lawn should be mown at least three or four times early in summer, or it may be kept short by turning in, a part of the time, a flock of sheep, when they can be easily seen, and injury to the trees prevented. The fruit garden may be kept cultivated by a shallow plowing early in spring, and a few harrowings afterwards, and perhaps one or two rollings near the season of fruit, to keep it smooth to the pickers. The ice-house, henhouse, and other of the smaller buildings, may be placed near the carriage-house. An evergreen hedge or screen separates the kitchen garden from the front grounds. A water reservoir and hitching posts, are placed at the right of the house, at the intersection of the roads. —*The Register of Rural Affairs*, 1871

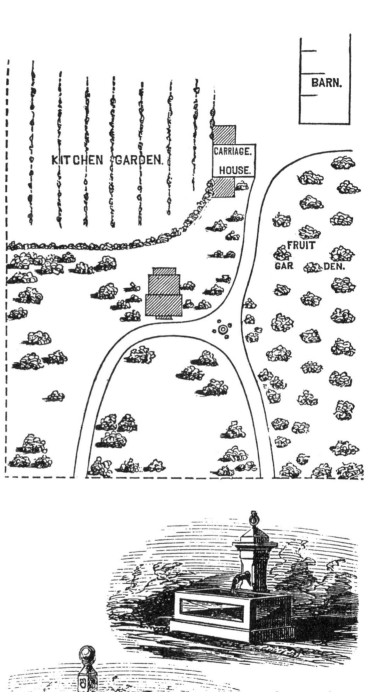

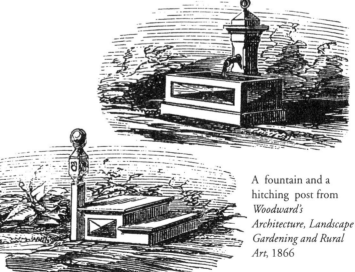

A fountain and a hitching post from *Woodward's Architecture, Landscape Gardening and Rural Art*, 1866

Where Ought the Farmhouse to Stand?

The building ought to stand where the farm roads and cart paths can conveniently concentrate and all approach by reasonably short and direct lines from the outlying fields. Steep pitches should be avoided even by making circuits, and the steepest places in the roads should be where loads will seldom be hauled up them. The heaviest loads of produce come from those fields upon which the most manure is hauled, so the buildings should be nearly on a level with the best land, or that which is most susceptible of high manuring and culture. Proximity to the highway is a great convenience, hence those farms are favored which are intersected by a public road. Where there is much travel, this having a constant troop of strangers and pilferers passing through one's grounds would be anything but desirable; but where the travelers would be chiefly neighbors and friends the case is reversed. In districts where strong fences must be maintained along the highways to prevent the trespassing of neighbors' cattle, preference may be given to such a location of the farm with reference to highways as will require least fencing.

In regard to views, the extensive panoramas obtained from hill-tops are not by any means so beautiful and pleasing to cultivated taste as the more limited landscapes, combining striking features both near and far, which are much more likely to be found at less exalted and more protected situations. A southern, southeastern, or east-south-and-west exposure, protected from northern and north-western winds by hills or forests is to be chosen, and extensive views of the grounds of others are to be regarded entirely subordinate to the ability conveniently to overlook one's own farm and laborers. —The American Agriculturist, 1864

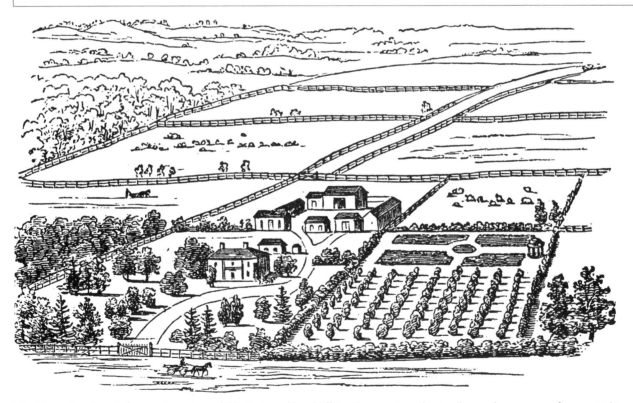

The illustration above is from an 1857 issue of *The Register of Rural Affairs*. Compare it to the site plan on the next page, from an 1867 architect's plan book, and you'll see how similar some farm folks' landscape ideas were to the high-style ideals of the day. Both layouts feature park-like grounds at the house. On the other hand, fenced fields, orchards and kitchen gardens all have a geometric grid for easy tillage and maintenance. Kitchen gardens on both drawings show an elegant, formal plan that's more like the gardens of the previous century than the "modern" naturalistic style of the day. Most views published in the 19th century show the same mix of styles in farmstead plantings.

E. A. Baumann and George E. Woodward, Architect, *Woodward's Cottages and Farmhouses*, 1867

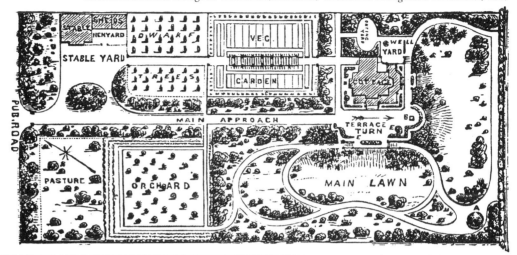

A Neat Front Yard Only

Persons of moderate pretensions, including a large portion of such as live on medium-sized farms, fall into another error. They devote to ornamental planting a square plot of ground exactly in front of the dwelling, and varying from half an acre down to two rods square. This is enclosed with a picket fence in the form of a tight pen, with one straight walk passing through the center from the front door down to a small gate opening into the public highway. Very few ever pass through this gate or enter through the front door; but carriages, wagons, and foot passengers go in at the large gate just without this square yard, and enter the house by a side or back door. The square yard is therefore often allowed to grow up with grass or weeds, and is shaded by a few cherry trees, one or two lilac bushes, and a few hollyhocks. Occasionally it is seen in much better order, with a straight and neatly-kept gravel walk lined with shrubs and flowers, and with rows of cherry and pear trees on either side— This is, however, the only neat portion of the whole premises; for the worm-fence enclosures on the right and left, and the back yard, contain a numerous collection of cord-wood, old rails, empty boxes, barrels and barrel hoops, unburned brush, plows and sleds, wagons and carts, pails and kettles, chips, slop puddles, &c. It appears, however, like a neat and comfortable residence to the traveler who is careful to look at it only at the moment when he is exactly in front. —John J. Thomas, The Register of Rural Affairs, 1860

Ornamental Planting

John J. Thomas, *The Register of Rural Affairs*, 1860

Country homes are of two kinds, the repulsive and the beautiful. The former are occupied by those who know nothing of domestic enjoyment, and who seek happiness in the bar room and grog-shop. They never see any charms in the works of nature. Ornamental shrubbery to them is "brush," and flowers are only "weeds." They never plant a rosebush nor a shade tree. They sometimes set out a few apple and cherry trees. But these are left to take care of themselves. They have an especial contempt for all ornamental trees, and exclaim, "What! set out trees that don't bear anything fit to eat, that are only good to look at!" Their dwellings are bleak and desolate. There is nothing about them attractive to their children, who grow up with no attachment to home, and with little appreciation of the social virtues. The first figure on this page is a representation of all that is inviting in the homes of their childhood, and where from the earliest dawn of their forming minds, they have received most of their impressions of life. Few of them have been able to surmount these discouraging influences, and they have become coarse and unintelligent. How different might have been their character if they had been brought up under the influences of the other home represented!

The neat cottage cost no more in the first place than the dilapidated one. Its owner kept it in perfect repair, and planted and cultivated the encircling grounds during those spare moments that his neighbor who lives in the other, occupied at the tavern. Each house cost nearly a thousand dollars in building; while the planting and cultivation of the grounds about the latter, did not require an expenditure of fifty.

Much money is wasted in attempts to ornament with all the assistance that may be derived from the experience of others. Those who wish to understand the subject completely are referred to Downing, Sargent, and Kemp, for full instructions; but a short article like this may perhaps afford many useful hints to those who cannot give so much time to the subject, or whose moderate grounds and limited means may not warrant great expenditure. In offering suggestions on this subject, it will be best to begin at the beginning, and lay down briefly a few rules for selecting a site for a dwelling.

The following requisites may be regarded as important nearly in the order in which they are named but some will transpose them more or less, according to their preferences: 1. Healthfulness, 2. Neighborhood, 3. Soil and climate, 4. Suitable site, convenience of access, &c., 5. Scenery and views. The first is all-important, as no home comforts can atone for ruined health. The second is scarcely inferior, for a family possessing civilization and refinement cannot properly enjoy themselves when constantly exposed to the petty annoyances of vulgar and pilfering neighbors, and who are shut out entirely from the social enjoyment of such as are of a congenial character. Where a whole neighborhood unites in works for public benefit and moral improvement, the very atmosphere seems purer and more delightful, than where semi-barbarism and selfishness are the ruling influences. A fertile soil is all-essential to the resident who would obtain the necessaries and comforts of life from his own land; and a climate favorable to the cultivation of the finer fruits is equally so to every one who expects to enjoy a constant circle of these most wholesome and delicious luxuries. The site, and suitable conveniences for access, are important considerations. A low, foggy place, will be unhealthful; a high one, without shelter, will be bleak and cold; if very near a public road, it will be exposed to noise, dust, and obtrusive observation; if remote from the road, much needless traveling will be required, and not a little inconvenience will be found in time of deep snows. A gentle eminence, and a moderate distance from the public road, and the shelter of evergreens on the side of prevailing winds, will obviate most of these difficulties. A quiet side-road branching from a main highway, will often be better than directly on a great thoroughfare. Comparative nearness to places of public worship, to schools, a post-office, mill and railroad station, are each of considerable importance, and should all be taken into consideration. The value of fine scenery will be variously estimated; some would prize it as all-essential, while others would scarcely think of it. Some would merely covet a showy situation as seen from the nearest highway, in order to draw the admiration of travelers; others, discarding such motives, would only desire beautiful views from the windows of the dwelling or from the surrounding grounds, in order to make their homes interesting and attractive to their children.

The site having been selected, the next step is to build the house. This portion of labor does not belong to our present subject, but the plan and intentions should be well understood before the exact spot for the house is fixed upon, and its frontings determined. This precaution is essential in order to secure the finest views, and to furnish protection from winds, or from undesirable odors or unsightly objects.

Great progress has been made within a few years in the art of ornamental planting, but it is still common to witness defects. The most common error of past years, but now rapidly disappearing, is the practice of planting only in straight lines or geometric figures. Absolute stiffness reigned supreme, in the attempt to avoid any approach towards irregularity. A neighbor, intelligent in other things, when he saw the first specimen of the natural mode of planting, exclaimed, "Why Mr. T.! you have none of your trees in rows!" He considered a want of straight lines a striking evidence of a bungler. The geometric style not only required this formal regularity, but symmetry, as it was termed, demanded that every object should have its corresponding one. A tree on one side must oppose just such a tree on the other side; a row on the right was to have its accompanying row on the left. It is stated that the old gardener of the Earl of Selkirk, was so strongly imbued with this mania for symmetry, that when he shut up the thief who stole his fruit in one summer-house, he was compelled for the sake of symmetry, to put his own son in the other opposite. How immeasurably more pleasing and beautiful than this stiff and artificial mode, is the simple imitation of the beautiful and picturesque in nature, which constitutes the modern or natural style of planting.

It is not an unfrequent error to suppose that the modern style consists merely in irregularity. But irregularity without arrangement, is not taste. Confusion is not the beautiful in nature. The perfection of art consists in producing a pleasing effect, while the art which produced it is concealed from the eye of the spectator. The scenery which artificial planting produces, may appear to be the accidental arrangement of agreeable parts or objects; but it must really be the result of close study and a careful eye, in the same way that the roughly dashed work of a skillful painter, where every touch, rude and accidental as it may seem at first glance, is found on taking the whole together, to produce a most perfect and complete combination of different parts. And one great excellence of the modern style consists in its complete adaptation to all grades of residences. It does not require costly embellishments, nor a profuse outlay. The cottage resident may show as much skill in a tasteful simplicity, as the owner of the magnificent park in the disposition of his broad lawns and majestic forest trees.

Dwellings on Oblique Roads

A correspondent has a trapezoidal piece of land, which he wishes to lay out as a building lot, of three or four acres, the road passing it obliquely. He is in a quandary whether to have the house face the road at right angles, and stand crooked with his neighbors where the road is straight, or else set his house "skewing" with the road, and he asks for information.

This is a common dilemma wherever diagonal roads exist, and we have many such inquiries from owners of small places. The course to be pursued must accord with circumstances. If the general course of the road is in the direction indicated, for a long distance, and the house is to be quite near it, then place the house directly facing the road, and flank it well with trees planted rather closely, so that its skewing position will be obscured by the foliage from those points where it would not appear well, as we have indicated in Fig. 1. If the house is to be placed at a greater distance from the road, then let it face the finest views, nearly irrespective of the course of the road. Plant the grounds in the modern style, and with properly curved walks or roads, and the irregularity will not be at all out of place. Fig. 2 represents something of the character proposed.

In all designs of the kind it must be borne in mind that the dwelling is to face the most desirable or beautiful views, or objects of importance.

Too much respect is commonly paid to the public highway, which is often a place for rubbish instead of being made a handsome avenue. In many places cattle and swine are allowed to run in the roads, which they disfigure by their rooting or droppings. Brush and stone are often thrown into them in clearing adjoining fields. Some farmers place their farm buildings on the line of the road, and make it a receptacle of all kinds of a implements and scattered lumber. Roads kept in such condition are not entitled to the respect which is shown them, by foregoing fine distant views or lake prospects in order that the dwellings may stand square and respectfully toward them. When country residents shall all unite in keeping their roads smooth and even, clear of all rubbish, neatly mowed, and handsomely planted with trees, so that they may be as agreeable a place for promenade or riding as a landscape garden, then we would advise that they be regarded as one of the best objects for a dwelling to face. The labor of keeping them in this condition would not be greater than that required to deface them, as it obviously requires as much work to carry brush, stones, lumber, tools, &c., into the road, as to carry them out of it. We may suppose that a house is about to be built on an elevated spot, where there are four desirable points visible. One is a beautiful lake, another a distant village, a third a broad rich valley, and the fourth a street with rubbish and straggling animals. Shall we turn away from the first three in order to enjoy the last? —*The Register of Rural Affairs*, 1872

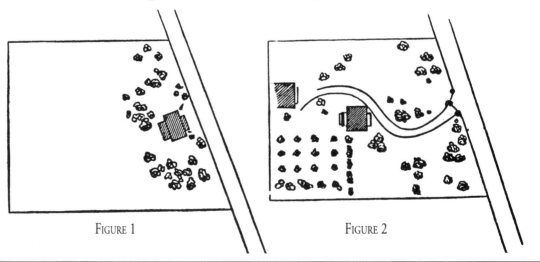

FIGURE 1

FIGURE 2

Laying Out Home Grounds

There are many farmers who desire to have their grounds about the dwelling laid out with some taste, but who cannot afford to keep up gravel walks, or to mow their lawns once a week. They would like a simple plan admitting the planting of shade trees, and the grazing of the grass by sheep or other animals, in lieu of mowing. Fig. 1 is intended to represent such a place, the entrance road having sufficient curve to remove all stiffness, and yet not so much as to give it a pretentious appearance. The common farm road lies on the left of these ornamental or shaded grounds, and both enter the yard devoted to the farm buildings at the rear.

A more finished plan is shown by Fig. 2, where the carriage-way has more curve, passes by the front entrance, and before entering the rear grounds, has a place for the turn of carriages. The lawn may be kept mowed, or be grazed short, as the owner may prefer. If mowed, a considerable portion of the small shrubbery may be planted near the dwelling, as shown in the plan; but if grazed, none but very large shrubs or small trees should be admitted. In planting the trees the owner will, of course, vary the places of the groups or belts, so as to have the most pleasing distant views open, and exclude any object of an undesirable or unsightly character. The farm road may lie at either side of these grounds. —*The Register of Rural Affairs,* 1873

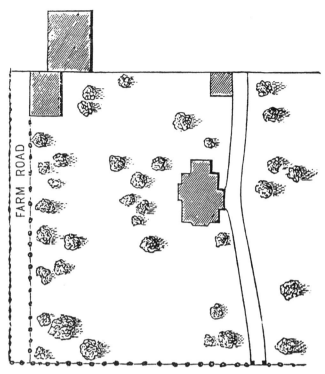

Fig. 1.—*Simple Plan of Farm Grounds.*

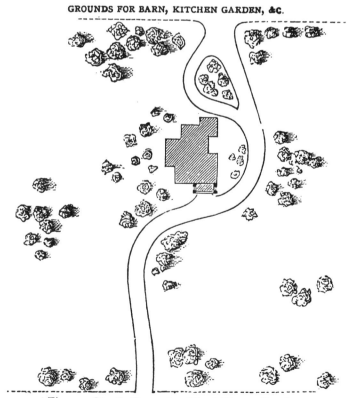

Fig. 2.—*Simple Grounds without Flower Garden.*

THE BALDNESS OF NEW PLACES

The remorseless manner in which the native trees have been totally cleared away from country residences, has left most of them in a very bleak and unsheltered situation. A neighbor had a natural oak grove before his house, but being strongly imbued with the cut-and-slash mania, chopped them all down, and then planted a row of maples in their place, which would require about thirty years to attain the size of the oaks. Sir Joshua Reynolds said he would paint Folly in the shape of a boy climbing over a high fence with an open gate close at his side. He might have done it more effectually by representing an American landowner cutting down all his native shade trees, that he might enjoy transplanted ones thirty years afterwards.

There are, however, many places where a thin natural growth of trees may be found, and among which a residence may be built. Yet with a most singular fatuity, such landowners avoid these beautiful natural parks, and build in an open field adjacent. We witness frequent instances of this folly.

Where trees have grown up thinly, their heads have become rounded and well developed, and nothing is easier than to remove those possessing the least beauty or which may stand in the range of fine landscape views. Even such as have grown closely together, and have shot up bare trunks, may be greatly improved in appearance in a few years, by heading them down soon after thinning out, as low as a good supply of side branches will admit, and gradually bringing them down into a fine form in successive years. The addition of other trees by planting, will soon greatly improve the appearance of the whole, and impart to the wildness and crudeness of nature, the grace and finish of an embellished landscape.

Where necessity leads to the selection of such places as have no trees, the most rapid mode of supplying the deficiency is, first to prepare the soil in the best manner by trenching or deep sub-soiling, at the same time working in large quantities of old manure or compost. Then plant moderate-sized, thrifty trees, which have been carefully taken up, and keep the soil bare and mellow for a few years, foregoing the pleasure of a green turf for the sake of a more rapid growth of the trees. Large trees when set out present a more conspicuous appearance at first, and some may be interspersed, but in a short period the smaller ones will have outstripped them, and will then present a richer, more dense, and far more beautiful foliage. By selecting a portion of the most rapidly growing sorts, as the Silver Maple, the European Larch, and the Abele, among deciduous trees; and the Norway Spruce, Scotch Pine and Austrian Pine, among evergreens a more speedy effect will be secured. —John J.Thomas, *The Register of Rural Affairs*, 1860

A COMPLETE COUNTRY RESIDENCE

John J. Thomas, *The Register of Rural Affairs*, 1858

Bringing together all the luxuries which a complete country residence may afford, with all the comforts and conveniences which may be combined in a single place, is of very rare but by no means difficult attainment. Such a place must comprise, besides the best household conveniences, trees and plants for the entire circle of fruits; a first-rate kitchen garden, for a full supply of the best early, medium, and late vegetables; fresh meat and poultry; and lastly, and by no means the least, the wholesome fascinations of ornamental planting.

The Ground Plan

The general design, and the relative size and position of each part, is readily understood from the accompanying plan of the whole. The portion of the farm covered by this plan, is about five acres. The house is seven rods from the public road. On the right are three-fourths of an acre devoted to ornamental planting; and on the left about the same is occupied with an orchard of standard pears. Immediately back of the ornamental grounds, is an acre devoted to dwarf fruit trees, currant, gooseberry and raspberry bushes, and to vegetables between the rows. Still further back is the fruit garden of standard trees, occupying nearly two acres.

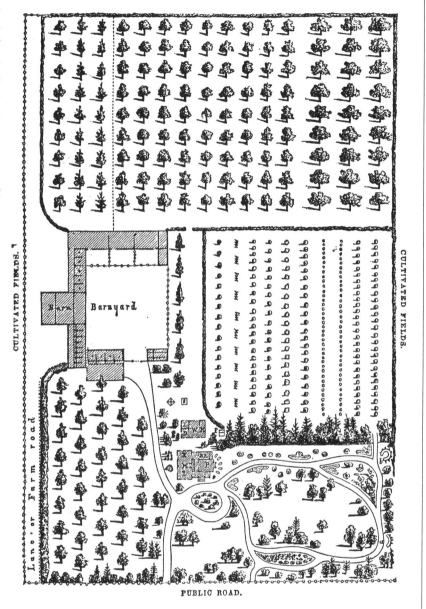

The best way to appreciate the variety of concepts and concerns that went into every country place is to see the design of a complete farmstead with farmhouse, outbuildings, landscaping and fields. The place shown above, and on the following pages was presented in 1858 by editor John Jacobs Thomas in his journal *The Register of Rural Affairs*.

Besides writing and editing, Thomas was a fruit farmer and a prolific designer. He seems to have penned dozens of buildings for his own farms, for neighbors and for tenants on his property in upstate New York. The buildings shown on this farmstead echo many designs that he submitted to other farm journals.

In writing about this place, Thomas gives specific costs of buildings and tells how high and how fast the trees and hedges grew. He was intimate with the workings of this place over many years. The designs for protecting orchards and storing fruit mirror concepts that he presented in his book *The American Fruit Culturist*. This is probably Thomas' own farm in Macedon, New York.

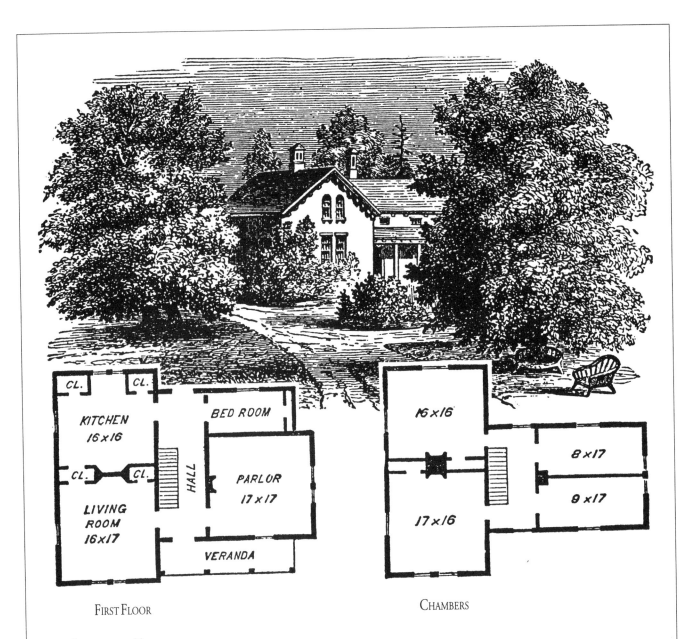

FIRST FLOOR

CHAMBERS

The Dwelling

The residence of which the plan is here given, includes no more than is within the reach of a large portion of farmers. The house is less in size than would satisfy many occupants; but the owner prefers to abridge his house-room by five hundred dollars in retrenchment, and expend this five hundred in fencing, ditching, deepening the soil and manuring his grounds; in planting fruit and ornamental trees; and in giving the whole that constant attention and culture, without which the best and most profitable results can never be reached.

The house fronts the south. There are three principal rooms and a bed-room below, and four bed-rooms above. The space, although small, comprises many conveniences. But little room is consumed by the hall, although it extends through the house, and affords every facility for ventilation in summer. No room is entered through another, but all open to the hall. The chimneys, being near the center of the house, economize the heat.

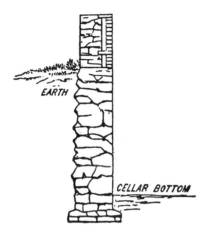

SECTION OF THE CELLAR WALL

The Cellar

Special attention has been taken with the cellar, as the safe and perfect preservation of the large supplies of apples and winter pears, and of winter vegetables, is a matter of great importance.

To secure the cellar from freezing, without the common disfigurement of banking up that portion of the wall above ground, is built double. The inner wall being brick four inches thick, with a space of air two inches, and an outer wall of stone fourteen inches thick, making twenty inches in all. The brick wall is stiffened by an occasional binder across to the stone; and the vacant space is filled with ashes. Tan or sawdust, or even sand, would have probably done nearly as well.

The cellar windows are all furnished with double sash for winter, admitting light, but not frost. The outer of these sashes, is removed as soon as the season for severe cold is past, and the inner one being hung on hinges, may be hooked up inside whenever fresh air is desirable. To prevent the ingress of anything from without, frames exactly the size of the outer windows, are made, and covered with wire netting; these replace the outer windows during warm weather.

Cottages

The house may seem too small, but as three cheap cottages have been built on another part of the farm, the hired men all board and lodge themselves, and no provision for accommodating workmen is necessary. The plan for one is shown.

This cottage was built of small frame timber, the two wings firmly bracing the central portion, four inch scantling being found quite large enough for this purpose. The plank siding formed the only connection in the frame between the plates and the sills, lessening the cost. The exterior is rough, and is occasionally whitewashed, obviating the expense of painting the large exterior surface.

KITCHEN 12 × 12

PRINCIPAL ROOM 16 × 16.

BED ROOM 11 × 11

VIEW ACROSS THE FLOWER GARDEN

The Ornamental Grounds

About three-fourths of an acre are devoted to the ornamental grounds. With the exception of walks and flower beds this is green turf. The ornamental grounds are most thickly planted towards the boundaries, where likewise there is a considerable proportion of evergreen trees interspersed, for the purpose of shelter.

The Pear Orchard

On the left or west side of the dwelling, is an orchard of forty standard pear trees, mostly of the autumn or winter sorts, early varieties not being so appropriate for so frequented a place. This pear orchard is protected from the west winds, and separated from the farm road, by a screen of Norway firs. Another screen, mostly of evergreens of several different species, to impart variety of appearance, separates the ornamental grounds from the dwarf fruit tree and kitchen garden. The inner line of this screen is straight and kept sheared; the outer is irregular in outline, to harmonize with the rest of the planting on that side. This screen forms a fine shelter on the north side of the flower garden.

The Kitchen Garden

The garden of dwarf fruit trees and vegetables is entered near the house, and also from the ornamental grounds at the summer house near b, through an arch made by training two trees together overhead. This garden occupies an acre.

The rows of dwarfs, running north and south, do not shade the plants growing between them, except an hour or two in the morning, and for the same length of time before sunset; and as dwarfs generally have very short and numerous roots, they do not operate as standard fruit trees in withdrawing nourishment from the soil for some distance off.

The strips of land between the rows of dwarfs are a rod wide, but only about ten feet are planted, leaving three feet next to the trees on each side. More than half an acre of actual space is thus allotted to the kitchen vegetables, which, with the exception of a few of the very smallest, are all planted in drills or double drills, and cultivated by horse labor.

This mode of cultivating is especially adapted to farmers' grounds, and not to small village gardens, where horse-labor cannot be so well applied, and is not easily obtained. It has another two-fold advantage; in manuring for vegetables, the dwarf trees get their share, so essential to success; and in cultivating the vegetables, the trees are not likely to be neglected.

The Fruit Garden

The fruit garden lies immediately back of the vegetable garden and farm buildings. Pigs and poultry are allowed to run freely in this fruit garden during the season of the setting and growth of the fruit to destroy all the fallen and wormy fruit. More room is given in the fruit garden to the apple than to other trees, by placing the rows wider apart, without disarranging the rows in both directions, or preventing the free cultivation of these trees by horse labor, so essential to their healthy growth, and to the quality of the fruit. A large orchard of winter apples grows on a more remote part of the farm.

The Hedges

The fruit garden, and the dwarf and vegetable garden are both surrounded with an excellent Osage Orange hedge, which no fruit-stealer can pass.

VIEW OF THE DWARF FRUIT GARDEN

END VIEW OF A PROPERLY TRIMMED HEDGE

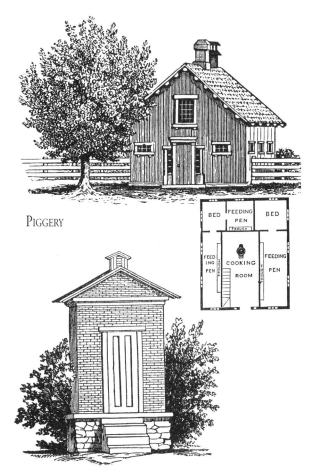

PIGGERY

SMOKE AND ASH HOUSE

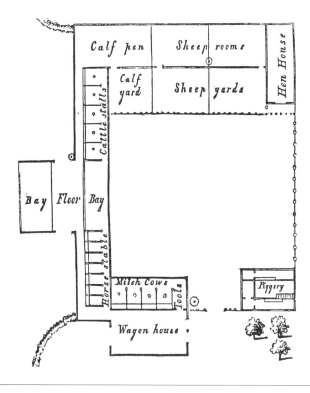

Outbuildings

Immediately behind the dwelling, and fifteen feet from it, is the building containing the wood-house, dairy and ice-house. The inconvenience of a separate wood-house, is balanced by the advantage of exclusion from the noise of cutting and sawing, which would be more annoying in immediate contact with a small house. The dairy, although fronting the south, is kept cool by several dense evergreen trees on its south-west corner, and by the ice-house in its rear.

The privy, P, is flanked by evergreen trees, and the passage to it is lined on both sides by Norway firs, which meet over head, and are kept sheared next to the path which it covers, thus forming at all times a sheltered green avenue.

The smoke-house is behind the ice-house. It is built of brick, with a stone basement for ash-pit, the latter being about four feet high, plastered smoothly with water-lime inside, and with a loose plank covering or floor, partly separating the ash-pit from the smoke-house above, and through which the ashes may be poured down. For smoking the meat, a fire is built on these ashes, where it may be perfectly controlled, and the smoke rises above. A ventilator surmounts the building, which is closed or opened at pleasure, to prevent the dampness so common otherwise with brick smokehouses, on the one hand; as well as a too free escape of smoke on the other.

Farm Buildings

The range of farm buildings is nearly explained by the annexed enlarged plan. The nearest corner is occupied by the piggery for convenience in emptying swill from the dairy and kitchen. A plan of this building is shown. The wagon-house, next on the left is forty feet long so as to afford ample shelter for wagons, carriages and other vehicles, which may be driven through, and out the opposite door. The barn itself is 30 by 45 feet, and is built on the usual plan, with a floor in the center, and bays on each side. It will be observed that teams may enter the barn and pass out the opposite side, from the farm road, with but a slight variation from its direct course.

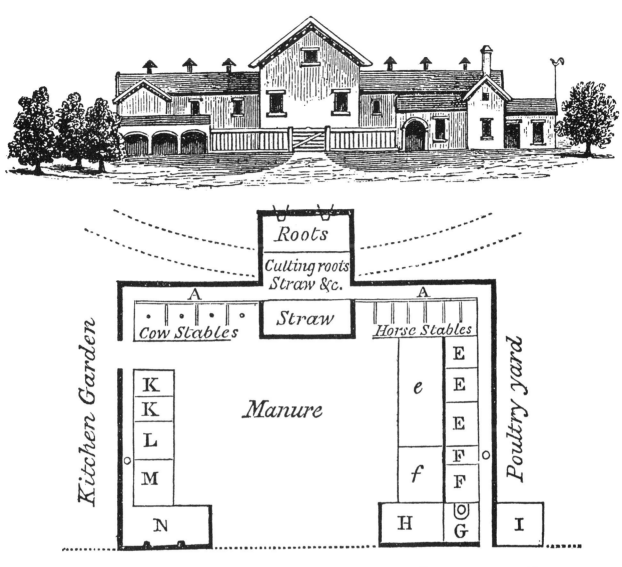

BARN AND STABLES

Two earlier designs by editor John J. Thomas give us a good idea of the appearance of the farm buildings on his 1858 farmstead shown in the plan on page 134. The view and plan above were published in his 1855 issue of *The Register of Rural Affairs.* Thomas noted that because of the arrangement, "those who have but limited means, may begin with a portion and add from time to time, as means and circumstances may warrant."

A-A is an access alley, E - sheep sheds, e - sheep yard, F -piggeries, f - pig yard, G - cooking house, H - wood shed, I - poultry house, K - calf sheds, L - workshop, M - tool house, N - wagon shed. The barn at the center of the plan is a traditional, side entry, English barn, with an entrance drive outside of the yard.

The elevation below was submitted by Thomas, with a similar plan, to *The Cultivator,* in 1844. That journal published the design in its May issue.

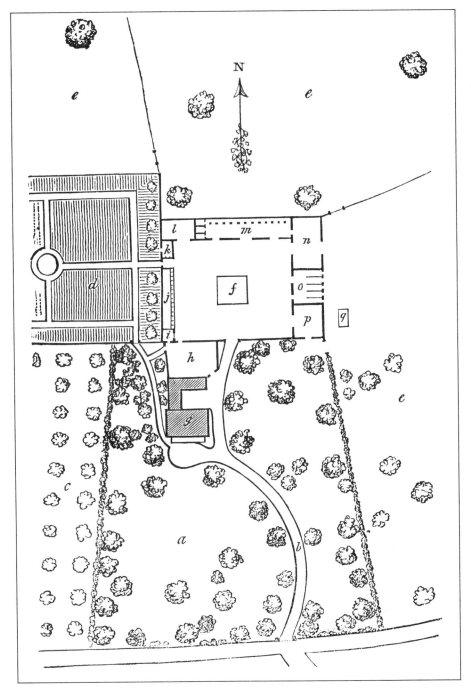

An Ornamental Farm

A.J. Downing, Architect,
Cottage Residences,
1842

The *ferme ornee* is a term generally applied to a farm, the whole or the greater part of which is rendered in some degree ornamental, by intersecting it with drives, and private lanes and walks, bordered by trees and shrubs and by the neater arrangement and culture of the fields. But it may also be applied to a farm with a tasteful farmhouse, and so much of the ground about it rendered ornamental, as would nat- the first time.

The annexed engraving is a plan of a few acres immediately surrounding the house, and consisting of the entrance lawn *a*, about one and a quarter acres, bordering the entrance road *b*; the orchard *c*, the kitchen garden *d*, adjoining fields, in grass or under the plow *e*, and the yard for outbuildings *f*.

At *g*, is the house, and in the rear of the kitchen, wash-house, & etc., is the kitchen yard *h*. The outbuildings, or farmery, are arranged around three sides of a square, open to the south, and consisting of the piggery *j*, the tool-house communicating with the garden *k*, open shed for carts, plows, &c., *l*, cowhouse with three calf pens attached at the end *m*, barn *n*, stable for horses *o*, wagon-house *p*, and a corn crib *q*. The surface of the yard descends slightly on all sides to the center where the manure heap is kept. This collection of outbuildings is much more complete and extensive than will be found connected with most farms in this country, but we have given it with a view of exhibiting what ought to be aimed at as a desideratum in accommodations, on every extensive farm; and it will be found easy to diminish the amount of buildings and sheds to as many as would occupy only one side of the yard, if the farm be small, or to such a number as can be afforded.

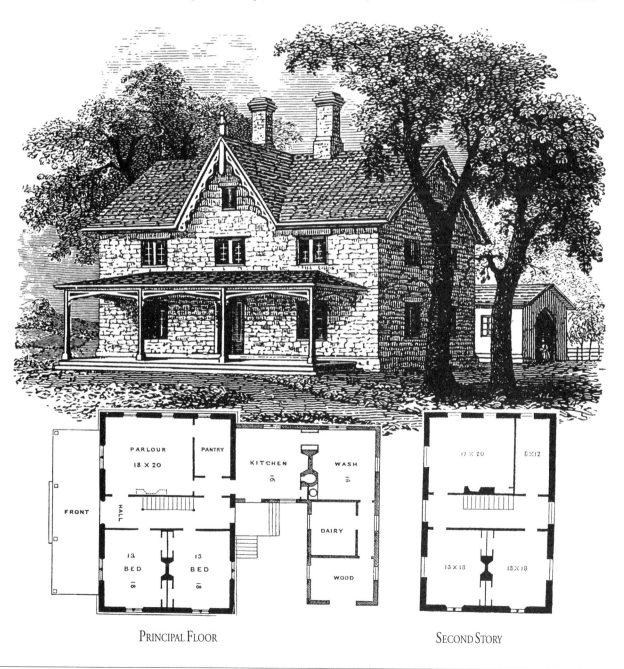

PRINCIPAL FLOOR   SECOND STORY

WELL

Stable

- 1, Tool Room
- 2, Poultry Room
- 3, Cow Stall
- 4, Feed Room

Yard

- a, Walk
- b, Stable Path
- c, Lawn
- d, Shrubbery
- e, Flower Bed
- f, Evergreen Screen
- g, Summer House
- h, Clothes Yard
- i, Fruit
- j, Vegetables
- k, Well
- l, Cow Yard
- m, Poultry Yard
- n, Piggery
- o, Manure Pit

Cottage

- V, Veranda
- H, Hall, 8.6 x 13
- P, Parlor, 13 x 18
- K, Kitchen, 13 x 14.7
- B.R, Bedroom, 8 x 13
- S, Scullery
- W.R., Wood Room

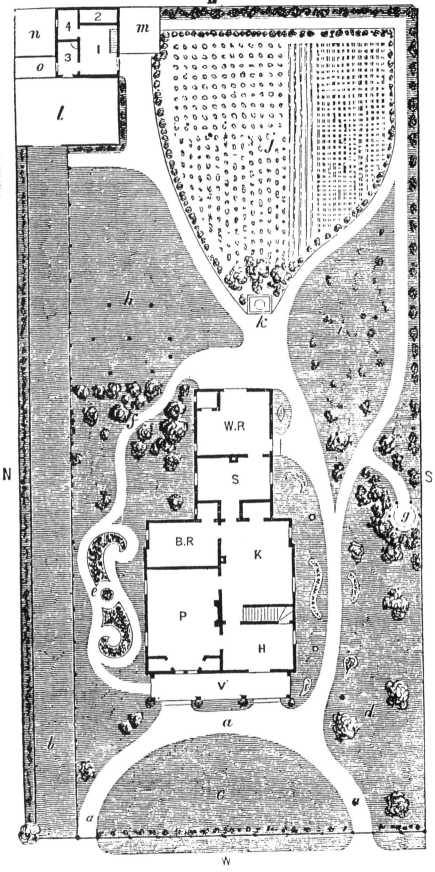

A Cottage and its Ground Plan

Henry W. Cleaveland, William Backus and Samuel D. Backus, Architects, *Village and Farm Cottages*, 1856

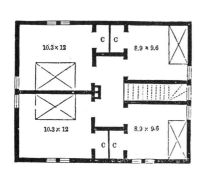

SECOND FLOOR PLAN

SUMMER
HOUSE

A New York Farmstead

The Register of Rural Affairs, 1857

The plan of Daniel T. More's farm, in Watervliet, New York shows the old geometric style of planting. The view, taken from the northeast, shows an old style Greek revival farmhouse and traditional barns and outbuildings. The engraver took some liberty with Mr. More's straight entry drive and gave it a more modern, graceful curve.

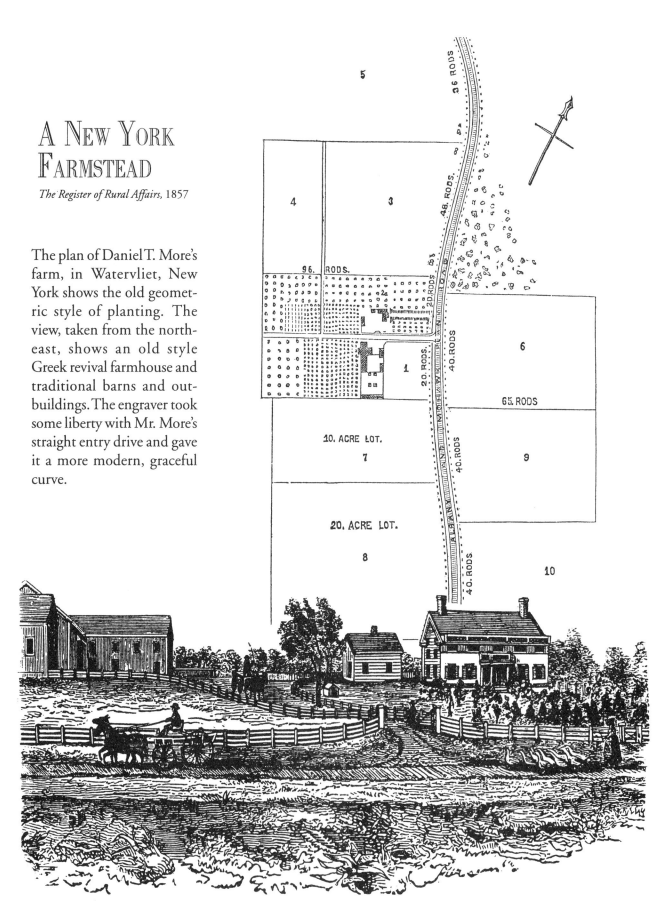

Chapter 8

Neighborhoods

THE IMPORTANCE OF COUNTRY NEIGHBORHOODS

Mrs. E.H. Leland, *Farm Houses In-doors and Out-doors*, 1881

A neighborhood is an excellent thing in the country. It is only the work-weary, noise-deafened, and perhaps slightly dyspeptic city-mind that ever sings in earnest of the charms of solitude, and; the all-satisfying companionship of nature. "If I must choose between men and trees," says a wise and witty somebody, "I must say that I prefer men." Transplant your weary city-ite to the quiet and solitude of some farm lying five miles from its little country post office, give him the sighing of the breeze and the chirp of the crickets night and day, with an Agricultural Report for reading, and the chickens and calves for companions, and in less than a year's time you will probably have on your hands a man gratefully ready to return to the cheerful activities and social advantages of his city home.

No one wants too much of anything, even of the serene, companionless quiet of a beautiful country region, and the happiest existence must be that which can command, along with green fields and singing streams, something of the good cheer and inspiration of congenial fellowship, both in social and business life.

A jocose city friend, who is more than half in earnest, however, says life can never possess its full meaning for her until she can have a fine fruit and dairy farm within ten minutes walk of the post-office! And so, while we recognize the stern fact that we cannot combine all the advantages of the city with all the beauty and freshness of the country, we can, in either situation, combine a little of the good in both.

It is characteristic of some farmers to jeer more or less at cities and city life, and to regard city people with a sort of derisive compassion. Visitors from cities to the country will grow familiar with such expressions as this: "So you've concluded to come out where

you can live for a while !" Now if farm people did but know it, it is an undeniable fact that, as farm life now is, it is in these same derided cities that one often lives most and lives best, providing one is not crushed within the narrow groove of poverty. While farmers shrug their shoulders at cities, let them remember that cities are drawing their sons and daughters away from them! That culture; society, and the pleasant clash and sparkle of immense business activities, often make lonesome, monotonous farm work very distasteful in comparison.

And whose fault is it that farm work is lonesome and monotonous? Certainly not the fault of the children born to it. Nor can the trouble be attributed to Dame Nature, who has given such lavish materials for beautiful homes. If farmers want to fortify their lofty position in regard to real "living," and if they want to keep their children near them, they must make an effort to lighten the lonesomeness and the monotony, and to create homes from which the children will not glide away as they grow older.

Let them try, among other things, the neighborhood cure. Half a dozen families, settled in neat houses within "calling" distance of each other, with spacious fruit and flower gardens, snug barns and granaries, and a single wide street adorned with shade trees and neat walks, would form a community richly productive of good. And what a charming contrast it would be to the same number of houses strung lonesomely a mile or more apart!

In the West, where land lines are drawn with geometric precision, and the comparative newness of the country makes the plan easily practicable, it is a wonder that farm neighborhoods have not sprung naturally into existence. Four "forties," or four "eighties," or even larger farms, touching each other at a central point, might have all their houses, barns, and other buildings collected in a social and picturesque little settlement at this center. The crossroads running through, might be set with shade trees, and fenced with neat and thrifty hedges. It would not be a great expense to make narrow gravel or flag walks on either side of these streets, with pretty rustic gateways leading into the grounds of each home. In the center of the small square formed by the intersecting roads, a well might be sunk, and a pump placed, shaded by a light rustic roof, and provided with drinking-cup and trough. Enough blessings, both from man and beast, would descend upon such an effort, in even one hot and dusty summer day, to pay the cost of it. One of these corner homes might maintain a good croquet ground; another, a capital swing large enough to send fathers and mothers into the air, as well as their children. Another could furnish a smooth and capacious stretch of turf for football and other games; while the ambition of the remaining corner might perhaps unfold beautifully in a comfortable and pleasant reading and club-room, where, in long winter evenings, the little community might gather sometimes for the reading and discussion of things of interest.

An attractive nucleus like this once formed, a portion, at least, of the sons and daughters growing up would be apt to build homes near at hand, and so the growth and beauty of the neighborhood would increase rather than diminish under the touch of the swift years.

Where four or five friendly families are gathered together, it would be no great task for some one of the fathers to collect the children, in winter weather, into a generous sleigh box (I would suggest plenty of sleigh-bells and warm robes), and take them to school, some other father going for them at night. The dreariness and inefficiency of the average country school is bad enough without subjecting children to the added misery of wading through miles of snow, and facing biting winds in order to reach its portal.

Many more or less important advantages would spring from such a community. Each family subscribing for one or two first-class magazines and newspapers, a profitable "circulating library," full of instruction and entertainment, would be the result. Clothes, groceries, and farm supplies, could be purchased at wholesale rates, and divided according to individual orders. Some happy boy, with a pony and stout leather satchel, could be chosen mail-carrier to and from the, perhaps, distant post-office, and there would follow the luxury of a daily paper for the reading room and letters delivered at the door.

A blacksmith's forge might be maintained, and save many trips to the village for simple repairs. A large easy wagon and four horses could occasionally convey the lecture or church-going portion of these families to town, when there should be something spe-

cially worth hearing; and the same vehicle would be fine for picnic expeditions and harvest frolics. A good sermon, out of the many now reported in the newspapers, might be selected for reading at some neighbor's house on rainy or snowy Sundays; and it would be strange if, even in so small a village, there might not be an organ and two or three good voices for the accompanying hymns. Such things do good, sometimes more good than is obtained in some stately church, with its imposing fashion and formality. Sewing-bees might be held, and the women expeditiously help each other through the hurry of spring and fall sewing. Husking-frolics and Wood-sawing Socials would occur; and what to both men and women is often hard and monotonous drudgery, would prove almost a recreation, because of the good cheer of humanity's helpful and inspiring companionship.

Such a neighborhood would be worth while, if only for its interchange of friendly lights on a stormy December night! What mother's heart but would beat braver as she rocks her sick baby in her arms, to know that three minutes distant, were other mother-hearts ready with their sympathetic aid and worthy counsel?

What children but would grow up happier, and better, and more intelligent from having dally companionship with other happy, good, and intelligent children?

What man but would enjoy and profit by the neighborly chat over farm matters, and political aspects, the neighborly help and the pleasant competition in making neat and thrifty homes?

A Neighborhood Plan

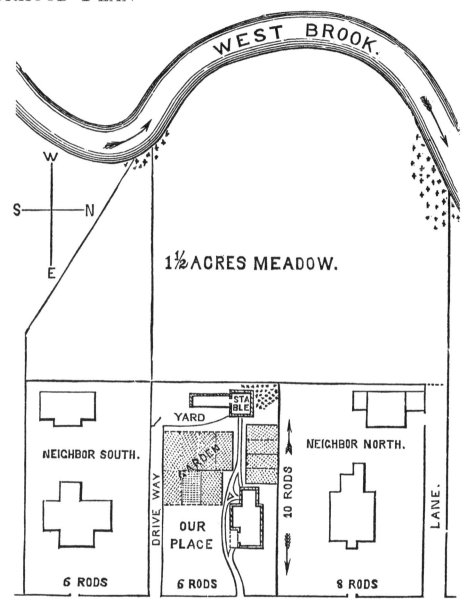

This plan, from Col. Mason Weld's 1880 book, *Keeping One Cow*, shows us the remarkable restraint that neighborliness had on country builders. The homes have a common setback from the road and are set at polite distances from their property lines at the sides and back.

Unwritten community standards for materials and paint colors were also adopted. First-hand views by painter Joseph Hidley in the 1860s, in rural Poestenkill, New York, show an orderly procession of white houses, taverns and churches close to village roads, red barns and service buildings set back from those and unfinished, weathered outbuildings further back still. A decade later in Wisconsin, farmer and painter Paul Seifert depicted his village and his neighbors' farms with a similar cadence.

Today we depend on zoning ordinances to define standards of finishes and building setbacks. Yesterday, courtesy was enough.

Neighborly Houses

An evil, which is becoming common, is expensive building. In riding lately through the suburbs of one of our cities, a resident informed us that a large portion of the prominent men of the place had failed, or become embarrassed, through the desire to excel their neighbors in splendid residences. We are not sure that our writers on this subject are not partly at fault in this particular. We have just looked through four American works, published within a few years - works whose leading characteristic ought to be republican simplicity - and find in one, (Downing's,) many country houses varying in cost from seven to ten and ten to fourteen thousand dollars, and another, (the most expensive,) with the cost not given. In the "Homes for the People," (Wheeler's,) there are a considerable number ranging at nearly all sums from ten to thirty thousand dollars; while the average of all, including even the log dwellings, is six thousand. Another recommends a four-story ten thousand dollar cottage (!!) for its cheapness; and the fourth work, less faulty than the others, has several designs for farm houses costing from four to eight thousand.

"But if the wealthy are able to build such houses," we are told, "let them build accordingly." By no means, we would say - for every man, as a patriot and a Christian, has a duty to perform to the community, during his rapid passage through the world; and if he sets an example of extravagance for his poorer neighbors, which they, in their desire to be "as good as their betters," are led improperly to follow, he is effecting a positive and serious evil. Many of the hard struggles and heavy debts of young heads of families, arise from the wish to be equal with their friends in their fine rooms, costly carpets, and silver furniture. We question if any man, however rich, has a right to build a ten thousand dollar dwelling, with these influences in view, when comfortable simplicity would be so much better than showy luxury; and the expenditure of means in the purchase of books and scientific apparatus, in the dissemination of knowledge and in promoting the substantial welfare of the world at large, would be better than the indulgence of the feeling that is expressed in the language, "Soul, thou hast much goods laid up, and a very fine house indeed to keep them in—enjoy it, and let others admire."

A disposition to copy extravagance runs through all ranks. Hence the great number of examples where farmers have built large houses and run themselves in debt, so that they could neither conduct their farming operations to advantage, nor make improvements by planting. There have been multitudes of instances where houses costing three thousand dollars have used up every available resource, when a cheaper erection of two thousand would have supplied as well every real want, and left a surplus of one thousand, a fifth part of which would have embellished the place by planting, furnished a profusion of comforts in the form of fine fruits, and in the end rendered the home not only more comfortable in every respect, but really of more moneyed value than the bleak three thousand mansion, with its broken fences and bare walls.

Our object is to encourage those of large means, instead of throwing their money away on luxuries, to show that although they can build showy houses, they prefer something that shall leave the world better than they found it. We should delight to set our eyes upon the man, who, with a hundred thousand dollars or more at command, would be willing to live in a dwelling worth two thousand, that he might have ampler means for the benefit of his race. —The Register of Rural Affairs, 1856

Chapter 9

Yesterday & Today

We move from cities and suburbs and build in the country partly because we love the look of countryside. It's ironic that the process of our construction is changing that look dramatically. It's hard to categorize the visual appeal of country villages and fine old farms, so it's very difficult to replicate their charm. I've designed homes that I thought would weave right into the fabric of their countryside and was disappointed. Part of my purpose for this book was to find those elusive qualities that might help improve my work. I hoped that by looking at the same designs that inspired yesterday's country builders and understanding their methods, I might gain some insight.

At first I looked for style and design. I have the same prejudices that yesterday's architects had. But, there are fine old country places in all styles and with or without elaborate details. There are many build-

ings with remarkably awkward proportions that are graceful in their country settings.

On a country road in upstate New York, I found an A.J.Downing cottage nestled in the trees. It is very pretty. There is a simple country church and some common cottages and barns in the same neighborhood. They were designed by people with less flair than Downing and less care for proportion and detailing. They looked every bit as good.

Age itself is not the charm. Weathered barns can be stunning, but so can well kept ones. I saw an 1879 painting by Wisconsin farmer, Paul Seifert. It was a view of a farmstead with a barn that I recognized from a farm journal plan. I've seen the same barn design, with a hundred years of weathering, in New York and New England, but in the painting, it was new and just as pretty.

Throughout this book I've asked you to look for what was common to all the designs. We found common plans but just a few common visual elements in the buildings. And yet Seifert's Wisconsin farm would look fine in Vermont. Unless there is a distinctive landscape, I have a hard time telling a photo of a 19th century Texas farm from one in Pennsylvania or a country village in Oregon from one in Virginia. What they have in common must be the key to the charm they share.

Page back through this book. I didn't plan it, but all of the views that show more than one building show those structures square with each other; roof ridges are parallel or perpendicular. That's true of all the site plans too, high-style or farmer drawn. I found seven more of Seifert's Wisconsin scenes. It's the same. Of 74 village and farm buildings in his paintings, 68 are rendered T-square straight with their road and with each other.

Look at country calendars or postcard views or some of those beautiful photos in coffee table books on barns. They all show that clusters of old country buildings were usually built squarely.

We saw that yesterday's book farmers loved order in their lives. That shows through in how they placed their structures. Since they built so much in our country's boom and since they built countrywide, it's their patterns that we still see. Americans built differently, more haphazardly, before their time, and we build very differently now.

Today when we build in the country, we plot our homes where we want them to be. Our site plans start as a clean sheet of paper or a blank computer screen. We find the spot that has the site's best combination of view, soil and access. Then we face the house to take advantage of the view. If the site is hilly, we usually grade it so the house and the garage are on the same level. Or, we might bend the house to follow a level area of the site. We might also angle the garage to make an easier entrance from the drive.

If there are zoning ordinances that limit our plans, we might try to bend them, too. Everyone today seems to want a variance.

Last century's builder always had limits on where a home could be placed. Houses were built where they had to be. The limits were set by custom and tradition. Unwritten standards like that were actually more stringent and effective than today's codes because they were unquestioned and freely accepted. There was no authority to grant a variance, but few wanted to vary. Neighborliness required that the setback from the road be similar to the adjacent homes. Tradition held that the home face the road and that all buildings or ells on the farmstead or in the neighborhood be square with each other.

There is an accidental elegance to buildings when they are placed and built the way they were. The old buildings enhance our appreciation of the countryside, and nature improves the appearance of the buildings.

The square order of a cluster of buildings or farm fields contrasts with the amazing disorder of nature. The contrast magnifies the visual attributes of each. The countryside's immeasurable variety and distance, the tangle of colors and the drama that weather performs in the sky are seen against the solid simplicity of what was built. The square-edged frame of a painting focuses our attention on the art. The square edges of the old buildings are the frames of nature's art.

Without today's easy way of moving earth with power equipment, yesterday's buildings were set close to the natural level of the ground, even if they were a good bit higher or lower than each other. Buildings set like that tend to show off the undulations of their site. A country hill will seem higher and a valley lower when dotted with houses and barns because windows and doors are a visual scale that we, unconsciously, measure the slope against. Again, the old buildings augment our view of nature.

On the other hand, hills and valleys can turn even slapdash structures into the art that the old architects promised. I thought that 19th century common homes in mountain regions had steeper roof angles than usual. I reasoned that their builders had responded practically to heavy snow loads. I was wrong; the roofs have the same range of pitches as flatland houses built in the same time period. My eyes were tricked by the same magic that nature uses to adapt the old buildings to the landscape.

Continued, page 150

Each of these country places is in a different state, yet they could look fine in the same neighborhood. They share a simple charm. Photos by Christopher J. Berg and the author.

In a perspective drawing of a building, setting the focal point or eye level low causes vertical dimensions to be exaggerated. A good renderer can make a dull building look dramatic by dropping the horizon line. The same thing happens in rolling country. If we look up at a structure, from a low focal point, it will appear higher than it really is and, if it has a peaked roof, that will seem steeper. Nature makes buildings in the mountains look steeper and so automatically blends them with her shapes.

Valleys are the reverse. Even a steep building seems flat and nestled in its site when seen from above.

The old common use of gable roofs, the old way of clustering buildings together, and construction in stages so that each building appeared as a cluster, added to the illusion. Simple gable-ended buildings show their roof angle best. With a multiple of gables all pushed down or stretched up to complement their natural setting, the visual effect is multiplied. What is accident seems perfectly planned. The mountainside farmstead reflects the drama of its mountain; the village below looks as peaceful as its valley.

Since yesterday's country folk tended to match their neighbors' homes in material and color as well as orientation and setback, whole neighborhoods looked as one. White paint, then common for all styles of country houses, blanched the details and made even the most ornate designs seem simple. White paint blended the styles from building to building on a farm and from farm to farm in a neighborhood. Red paint did the same for barns. Both colors were strong contrasts with the tones of the landscape, and both made gables and their angles stand out boldly against their settings.

Farmers and country carpenters created places that have held their beauty for generations. Their most consistent visual elements were gables, good order and a good coat of paint. Making a fine-looking American country place may be as simple as setting a few white gabled buildings square with each other and with the old farm next door.

Illusion helps fit simple buildings to their site. Buildings on a hill and seen from below seem taller and more angular, in keeping with hilly or mountainous country. The same structures, in a valley and seen from above, appear lower and seem to have gentler angles.

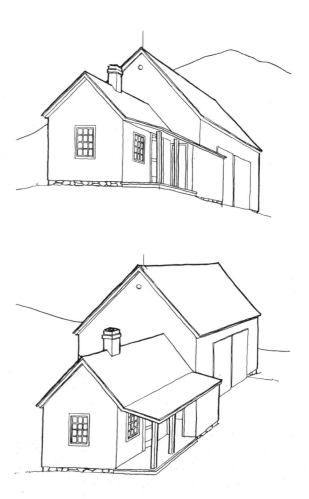

Chapter 10

An
American
Style?

Are the plans in this book the "American" homes that the farmers were looking for? American farms and country villages in New England look remarkably similar to ones in Oregon, the Carolinas and Kansas. Did the designs published in architects' plan books and farmers' journals add to that similarity?

The brightly painted, square-edged, proud 19th century farms that we still see in the countryside can hardly be recognized as descendants of rough subsistence homesteads or as siblings to the stylish homes of our cities. Did the country builders create their own style?

There is a common look to our country places: clusters of simple buildings collaged on a grid that birds can appreciate best; buildings aligned in plan but tumbling every which way in elevation; and bold, enveloping colors that stand out of the landscape. In addition, there are structural elements that appear fairly often in the designs in this book and in old rural homes. They include a steep, gable roof wi.h at least one gable wall raised to the height o. .he attic; a veranda; a raised basement; common, small-scale materials like clapboard, brick and fieldstone that give a delicate texture to plain surfaces; and little bits of fancy in detail accents at entrances and windows.

It's a well known concept that Americans concentrate their design efforts on the fronts of houses. The old designs in this book support that idea. Most ornament is near the front door. The backs of houses, and kitchen ells are the plainest. This carries through to barns and outbuildings which were usually set behind the house and have little ornamentation.

The designs also show that both professional and folk designers of the time experimented with their structures. Traditional solutions to spatial layouts were mixed with new concepts. Old center hall boxes were bent into L shapes or stretched with wings. The new, less formal shapes were infinitely more flexible than

Kitchens and kitchen living rooms were the center of family activity. They usually opened onto the farm work yard or the road.

Illustration from Will Carleton's *Farm Ballads*, 1873

the old boxes. These new homes could grow easily with new bays and ells.

As to a strong visual style, the way we architects try to define it, there is little consistency. Good country home plans might be draped in Gothic details. They might also be pure Italian or totally plain. The designs in this book are more stylized than most country buildings of the time. Remember that back then, just as now, it was innovations that were published; there was no reason to waste an expensive woodcut or engraving on what was commonplace. Old classic-style buildings and simpler regional ones continued to be built, side by side with these. The style that seemed to emerge was no true style but a careless amalgam of all.

Style was just not that important to yesterday's country builders. Time and again in their texts, they repeated what an editor of *The Cultivator* wrote in 1845: "The plan of a farm house is a matter of much consequence. Convenience and comfort are the prime requisites." It was the best plan that took the ribbon at the county fair. Style and ornament came later, if at all. Commonsense layouts are the core of common country buildings. When farmers sat down to design buildings they concentrated on the plans, so it's there we can best see their concepts and concerns.

The layouts of the published plans have many similarities. The front doors of country homes let guests into halls or parlors. Kitchens and farm offices often had their own entrances. Plans were efficient; there was little wasted space and few railroaded rooms. Families spent what leisure time they had together in one space. That space had different names over time. In

Published designs echoed the plan features and axial site layouts of the more traditional buildings of the time. This vernacular farmhouse, with classic Greek trim, was built near Belvidere, Illinois, in 1850.

Historic American Building Survey drawings from the Library of Congress.

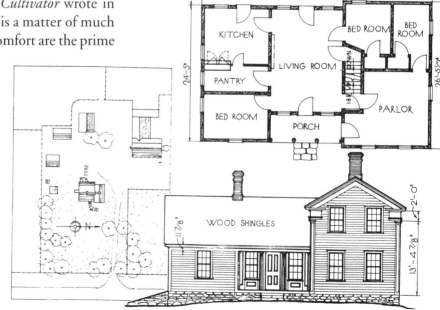

An extra bedroom near the kitchen served as nursery or infirmary. When not needed for that, it could be used by guests, farm hands and overnight boarders.

Illustration from the book *Farm Ballads*, 1873, by Will Carleton.

the plans in this book, it's called the sitting room, living room or dining room. It was always adjacent to the kitchen or one with the kitchen in small houses. In small houses the combination kitchen and family room was called a living room. In more opulent houses it was split into two adjoining spaces, usually called the dining and sitting rooms. That family space was usually more central in the home and larger than the parlor. Halls were for passage only and not the entertainment rooms popular on urban and high-style homes. Most of the homes had a ground-floor bedroom near the kitchen. Verandas were almost universal.

Kitchens were carefully planned. They tended to have easy access to the dining/living room, to any halls and to the outdoors. Cellar storage was usually reached by stairs from the kitchen. Pantries opened to the kitchen. On high-style homes of the time, they were usually entered from the dining room. Farm kitchens had washrooms and other workrooms attached. Site plans of farmsteads show that kitchens usually had views of the road and of the farmyard.

The plan features helped create the shape of the exteriors. Sometimes there was the magic that Michigan farmer B.W. Steere found in his designs when "beauty of proportion...harmonizes with what is most convenient and best for us." American country homes spread and ramble at ground level and are tighter and neater above. This anchors a house visually to its site and gives a look of permanence and solidity. Practical responses to the environment also helped the appearance. High room ceilings, tall windows, attic gables

This barn has an New England-style timber frame, a Pennsylvania-German stone cellar and a Dutch-style gable end entry. The little pent roof over the side doors was common to colonial-era German and Dutch barns. The small hinged wicket door set into the big rolling one is a detail that was popular in England. The idea of a bermed entry ramp may have been borrowed from an architect's plan book (see page 117). The wide roof overhang, cupola ventilators and round top vent are hints of Italian architecture. What style is it?

Barn design from Byron D. Halstead's *Barn Plans and Outbuildings*, 1881

and a raised basement helped keep the homes of the time cool and dry, but they also made them taller and more stately than earlier homes. Wide roof overhangs and big verandas gave shadows that contrasted nicely with the bright plain walls.

Kitchens were often in a separate wing or under a separate roof. This dissipated cooking heat and kept the rest of the house cooler. It also allowed the common practice of building a small first home, which remained as the kitchen ell when the family grew and more rooms were added. Although these published plans are dramatically different from most of the vernacular homes that preceded them, they include many common features like the kitchen ell. It's this weaving of old customs to the new, and regional ways to countrywide, that is a fascinating aspect of the time and of the designs.

The first-floor bedroom accommodated travelers but still functioned as the traditional "birthing room." The cellar for the new root crops was raised out of the ground in old Louisiana style. Most kitchens have a covered porch or stoop which served just like an old summer or bake kitchen when the new iron stove was carried out.

English heavy timber frames mixed with new, light Midwest stick framing. A fancy home created by an Ohio woman who never studied design might front a dairy barn designed by a New York architect who prob-

ably never studied farming. New factory-made metal tiles might clad old-style Dutch pent roofs on a barn with a German stone cellar. Like our language, food, religions and customs, we see America in the mix.

If these buildings don't make a common architectural style, they still form a fine national icon. We saw that the process of drawing plans helped country builders communicate with urban architects and how the designs that evolved combined both groups' ideas. Those designers, urban and rural, harmonized a world of building traditions.

We're a melting pot, aren't we? Our old country villages and farmsteads show that we once built very much the same over vast distances. We had a coast-to-coast community of ideas, a region based on lifestyle instead of state borders or those other borders that hem folks by their accents or their wealth.

Americans of dramatically different backgrounds, and different economic circumstances, once built very much the same. Young farmers and newly settled families of immigrants built a little house and small barn using the same elements and the same materials as their prosperous, long-settled neighbors. They painted them the same colors and expected them to grow to the same proportions. They made their plans and laid those buildings as the foundation of the same prosperity. Only time stood in their way. That's American, isn't it?

BIBLIOGRAPHY

Architectural Styles

Blumenson, John G. *Identifying American Architecture: a Pictorial Guide to Styles and Terms, 1600-1945.* New York: W.W. Norton & Co., 1981.

Foley, Mary Mix. *The American House.* New York: Harper & Row, 1981.

McAlester, Virginia and Lee. *A Field Guide to American Houses.* New York: Alfred A. Knopf, 1984.

Walker, Lester. *American Shelter.* Woodstock, NY: The Overlook Press, 1981.

Building History and Traditions

Benes, Richard, ed. *New England/New France: 1600-1850.* Boston: Boston University/The Dublin Seminar for New England Folk Life, 1992.

Brand, Stuart. *How Buildings Learn.* New York: Penguin Books, 1994.

Brent, Ruth and Benyamin Schwartz, eds. *Popular American Housing: a Reference Guide.* Westport, CT: Greenwood Press, 1995.

Carter, Thomas and Bernard L. Herman, eds. *Perspectives in Vernacular Architecture III.* Columbia: University of Missouri Press, 1989.

———. *Perspectives in Vernacular Architecture IV.* Columbia: University of Missouri Press, 1991.

Clark, Clifford Edward, Jr. *The American Family Home 1800-1960.* Chapel Hill: University of North Carolina Press, 1986.

Cohen, David Steven. *The Dutch American Farm.* New York: New York University Press, 1992.

Cronon, William. *Changes in the Land: Indians, Colonists, and the Ecology of New England.* New York: Hill and Wang, 1983.

Cummings, Abbott Lowell. *Architecture in Early New England.* Sturbridge, MA: Old Sturbridge Village, 1984.

Donald, Elsie Burch. *The French Farmhouse.* New York: Abbeville Press, 1995.

Drury, John. *Historic Midwest Houses.* Minneapolis: University of Minnesota Press, 1947.

Fitch, James Marston. *American Building 1: The Historical Forces That Shaped It.* Boston: Houghton Mifflin Co., 1966.

———. *American Building 2: The Environmental Forces That Shape It.* Boston: Houghton Mifflin Co., 1972.

Glassie, Henry. *Patterns in the Material Folk Culture of the Eastern United States.* Philadelphia: University of Pennsylvania Press, 1975.

———. *Folk Housing in Middle Virginia: A Structural Analysis of Historic Artifacts.* Knoxville: University of Tennessee Press, 1975.

Hamlin, Talbot. *Greek Revival Architecture in America.* New York: Oxford University Press, 1944.

Jakle, John A., Robert W. Bastian and Douglas K. Meyer. *Common Houses in America's Small Towns: The Atlantic Seaboard to the Mississippi Valley.* Athens: University of Georgia Press, 1989.

Nobel, Allen G. *Wood, Brick & Stone: The North American Settlement Landscape. Vol. 1, Houses.* Amherst: University of Massachusetts Press, 1984.

———, ed. *To Build in a New Land: Ethnic Landscapes in North America,* Baltimore: The Johns Hopkins University Press, 1992.

Pierson, William H., Jr. *American Buildings and Their Architects: Technology and the Picturesque, The Corporate and the Early Gothic Styles.* Garden City, NY: Anchor Press/Doubleday, 1980.

Pratt, Dorothy and Richard. *A Guide to Early American Homes.* New York: Bonanza Books, 1956.

Quiney, Anthony. *The Traditional Buildings of England.* London: Thames and Hudson, 1990.

Ritchie, Thomas. *Canada Builds.* Toronto: University of Toronto Press/ National Research Council of Canada, 1967.

Rushton, William Faulkner. *The Cajuns: From Acadia to Louisana.* New York: The Noonday Press, 1995.

Scully, Vincent. *The Shingle Style and the Stick Style.* New Haven: Yale University Press. Revised Edition, 1971.

———. *Architecture: The Natural and the Manmade.* New York: St.Martin's Press, 1991.

Stilgoe, John R. *Common Landscape of America, 1580-1845.* New Haven: Yale University Press, 1982.

Upton, Dell and John Michael Vlatch, eds. *Common Places: Readings in American Vernacular Architecture.* Athens: University of Georgia Press, 1968.

Vlach, John Michael. *Back of the Big House.* Chapel Hill: University of North Carolina Press, 1993.

———. "Greek Revival Architecture" and "Gothic Revival Architecture" in Mark P. Leone and Neil Asher Silberman eds. *Invisible America: Unearthing Our Hidden History.* New York: Henry Holt and Co., 1993.

Wells, Camille, ed. *Perspectives in Vernacular Architecture.* Annapolis, MD: Vernacular Architectural Forum, 1982.

———. *Perspectives in Vernacular Architecture, II.* Columbia: University of Missouri Press, 1986.

Farms and Farm Buildings

Benes, Richard, ed. *The Farm.* Boston: Boston University Press/The Dublin Seminar for New England Folk Life, 1988.

Hubka, Thomas C. *Big House, Little House, Back House, Barn: The Connected Farm Buildings of Rural New England.* Hanover, NH: University Press of New England, 1984.

Kauffman, Henry J. *The American Farmhouse.* New York: Hawthorn Books, 1975.

Larkin, David. *The Essential Book of Barns.* New York: Universe Publishing, 1995.

———. *Farm: The Vernacular Tradition of Working Buildings.* New York: Monacelli Press, 1995.

McMurry, Sally. *Families & Farmhouses in 19th Century America.* New York: Oxford University Press, 1988.

Nobel, Allen G. *Wood, Brick & Stone: The North American Settlement Landscape. Vol.2, Barns and Farm Structures.* Amherst: University of Massachusetts Press, 1984.

———. and Richard K. Cleek. *The Old Barn Book.* New Brunswick, NJ: Rutgers University Press, 1995.

Patterson, Emma L. *Munson Family Record.* Peekskill, NY. Unpublished history of the Munson family and farm, 1940.

Schuler, Stanley. *American Barns.* Atglen, PA: Schiffer Publishing, 1984.

Sloan, Eric. *An Age of Barns.* New York: Henry Holt & Co., 1967.

Folk and Popular Art

Bishop, Robert. *The World of Antiques, Art, and Architecture in Victorian America.* New York: E.P. Dutton, 1979.

———. and Jacqueline M. Atkins. *Folk Art In American Life.* New York: Viking Studio Books, 1995.

Gillon, Edmund V., Jr. *Pictorial Archive of Early Illustrations and Views of American Architecture.* Mineola, NY: Dover Publications, 1971.

Kogan, Lee and Barbara Cate. *Treasure of Folk Art from the Collection of the Museum of American Folk Art.* New York: Abbeville Press, 1994.

Lipman, Jean, Elizabeth V. Warren, and Robert Bishop. *Young America: a Folk Art History.* New York: Konecky & Konecky/The Museum of American Folk Art, 1986.

———. and Tom Armstrong, eds. A*merican Folk Painters of Three Centuries.* New York: Hudson Hills Press in association with the Whitney Museum of American Art, 1980.

Pratt, John Lowell, ed. *Currier & Ives: Chronicles of America.* New York: Promontory Press, 1968.

Simkin, Colin, ed. *Currier and Ives' America.* New York: Crown Publishing, 1952.

Vlach, John Michael. *Plain Painters: Making Sense of American Folk Art.* Washington: Smithsonian Institution Press, 1988.

Plan Book Architecture

Grow, Lawrence. *Old House Plans.* New York: Universe Books, 1987.

Gunter, Robert P. and Janet W. Foster. *Building by the Book.* New Brunswick, NJ: Rutgers University Press, 1992.

Hitchcock, Henry Russell. *American Architectural Books.* New York: DaCapo Press, 1976.

Hugo-Brunt, Michael. "Downing and the English Landscape Tradition," in A.J. Downing. *Cottage Residences.* Watkins Glen, NY: American Life Foundation. Reprint of the 1842 plan book, 1887.

Naversen, Keneth. *East Coast Victorians.* Wilsonville, OR: Beautiful America Publishing Co., 1990.

O'Neal, William B. "Pattern Books in American Architecture, 1730-1930" in Mario di Valmarana, ed. *Building by the Book.* Charlottesville: University of Virginia Press, 1984.

Schuyler, David. *Apostle of Taste: Andrew Jackson Downing, 1815-1852.* Baltimore: The Johns Hopkins University Press, 1996.

Shettleworth, Earle G., Jr. "Edward Shaw, Architect and Author" in Edward Shaw. *The Modern Architect.* Mineola, NY: Dover Publications. Reprint of the 1854 plan book, 1995.

Sweeting, Adam William. *Reading Houses and Building Books: Andrew Jackson Downing and the Architecture of Popular Antebellum Literature.* New York University doctoral dissertation, 1993.

Stilgoe, John R. *Borderland: Origins of the American Suburb, 1820-1939.* New Haven: Yale University Press, 1988.

Tomlain, Michael A. "Toward the Growth of an Artistic Taste" in George F. Barber. *The Cottage Souvenir, No.2.* Watkins Glenn, NY: American Life. Reprint of the 1891 plan catalog, 1981.

Upton, Dell. "Pattern Books and Professionalism: Aspects of the Transformation of Domestic Architecture in America, 1880-1860." *Winterthur Portfolio 19,* Nos. 2/3, Summer/Autumn,1984.

Van Dine, Alan. *Unconventional Builders.* Chicago: J.G.Ferguson Publishing, 1977.

The Times

Adams, James Truslow, ed. *Album of American History.* New York: Charles Scribner's Sons, 1945.

Benes, Richard, ed. *House and Home.* Boston: Boston University Press/The Dublin Seminar for New England Folk Life, 1990.

Berg, Donald J. *The Door Yard.* Berkeley, CA: Ten Speed Press, 1988.

————. *The Kitchen Gardeners' Guide.* Berkeley, CA: Ten Speed Press, 1987.

Countryman, Edward. *Americans: a Collision of Histories.* New York: Hill and Wang, 1996.

Hawke, David Freeman. *Everyday Life in Early America.* New York: Harper & Row, 1988.

Larkin, Jack. *The Reshaping of Everyday Life: 1790-1840.* New York: Harper & Row, 1988.

Leone, Mark P. and Neil Asher Silberman, eds. *Invisible America: Unearthing Our Hidden History.* New York: Henry Holt and Co., 1995.

Levine, Bruce, Stephen Brier, David Brundage, et.al., eds. *Who Built America?: Working People and the Nation's Economy, Politics, Culture, and Society.* New York: Pantheon Books, 1989.

Maas, John. *The Gingerbread Age.* New York: Bramhall House, 1967.

Sellers, Charles. *The Market Revolution: Jacksonian America, 1815-1846.* New York: Oxford University Press, 1991.

Sutherland, Daniel E. *The Expansion of Everyday Life: 1860-1876.* New York: Harper & Row, 1989.

Wolf, Stephanie Grauman. *As Various As Their Land.* New York: Harper & Row, 1994.

19th Century Sources

Allen, Lewis F. *Rural Architecture.* New York: C.M. Saxton Agricultural Book Publisher, 1852.

Atwood, Daniel T. *Atwood's Country and Suburban Houses.* New York: Orange Judd & Co., 1871.

Bailey, L.H. *Garden Making: Suggestions for the Home Grounds.* Norwood, MA: The Norwood Press, 1898.

Baker, Z. *Modern House Builder.* Boston: Higgins Bradley and Dayton, 1857.

Barber, George F. *New Model Dwellings and How Best to Build Them.* Knoxville, TN: George F. Barber & Co., 1894.

Bicknell, Amos J. *Bicknell's Village Builder & Supplement.* New York: A.J.Bicknell & Co., 1874.

————, ed. *Wooden and Brick Buildings with Details.* New York: A.J.Bicknell & Co., 1875.

————. *Specimen Book of One Hundred Architectural Designs.* New York: A.J. Bicknell & Co., 1879.

Birkback, Morris. *Notes on a Journey to America.* London: Severn and Company, 1818.

Brunner, Arnold W., ed. *Cottages or Hints on Economical Building.* New York: William T. Compstock, 1884.

Carleton, Will. *Farm Ballads.* New York: Harper Brothers, 1873.

————. *Farm Legends.* New York: Harper Brothers, 1875.

————. *City Ballads.* New York: Harper Brothers, 1885.

Cleaveland, Henry W., William Backus and Samuel D. Backus. *Village and Farm Cottages.* New York: D. Appleton and Co., 1856.

Comstock, William T., ed. *Comstock's Modern Architectural Designs and Details.* New York: William T. Comstock, 1881.

————. *American Cottages.* New York: William T. Comstock, 1883.

Downing, Andrew Jackson. *A Treatise on the Theory and Practice of Landscape Gardening.* New York: Wiley & Putnam, 1841.

————. *Cottage Residences.* New York: Wiley & Putnam, 1842.

————. *The Architecture of Country Houses.* New York: D. Appleton & Co., 1850.

————. *Rural Essays.* New York: G.P. Putnam & Co., 1853.

Flint, Charles L. *The American Farmer.* Hartford, CT: Ralph H. Park & Co., 1882.

Fowler, Orson Squire. *A Home for All: or, The Gravel Wall and Octagon Mode of Building.* New York: Fowlers and Wells, 1848.

Gay, William, ed. *Gay's Standard Encyclopaedia and Self Educator.* New Haven: William Gay & Co., 1882.

Halstead, Byron D. *Barn Plans and Outbuildings.* New York: Orange Judd Co., 1881.

Harney, George E. *Barns, Outbuildings and Fences.* New York: The American News Co., 1870.

Hill, Thomas E. *Hill's Manual of Social and Business Forms.* Chicago: Hill Standard Book Co., 1880.

Hobbs, Isaac H. and Son. *Hobbs's Architecture.* Philadelphia: J.B.Lippincott & Co., 1873.

Holly, Henry Hudson. *Holly's Country Seats.* New York: Appleton & Co., 1866.

Hussey, Elisha Charles. *Home Building*. New York: Leader & Van Hoesen, 1875.

Jacques, Daniel Harrison. *The House: A Manual of Rural Architecture*. New York: George Woodward, 1866.

King, David W. *Homes for Home Builders*. New York: Orange Judd Co., 1885.

Leland, E.H. *Farm Houses In-doors and Out-doors*. New York: Orange Judd Co., 1881.

Mitchell, Donald Grant. *Rural Studies*. New York: Charles Scribner & Co., 1867.

Munkittrick, Richard Kendall. *Farming*. New York: Harper & Brothers, 1891.

Palliser, George and Charles. *Palliser's Model Homes*. New York: Palliser, Palliser & Co., 1883.

Reed, Samuel Burrage. *House Plans for Everybody*. New York: Orange Judd Co., 1878.

———. *Cottage Houses*. New York: Orange Judd Co., 1883.

Robinson, Solon. *Facts for Farmers*. New York: A.H.Johnson, 1863.

Scott, Frank J. *The Art of Beautifying Suburban Home Grounds*. New York: D. Appleton & Co., 1872.

Shoppell, Robert W., ed. *How to Build, Furnish & Decorate*. New York: Co-operative Building Plan Association, 1883.

———. *Shoppell's Modern Houses*. New York: Co-operative Building Plan Association, 1887.

Sloan, Samuel. *The Model Architect*. Philadelphia: E.S.Jones & Co., 1852.

———. *Sloan's Homestead Architecture*. Philadelphia: J.B.Lippincott & Co., 1866.

Thomas, John J. *The American Fruit Culturist*. New York: William Wood & Co., 1875.

Thoreau, Henry David. *Walden*. 1897 Edition. Boston: Houghton, Mifflin and Company, 1854.

Todd, Sereno Edwards. *The Young Farmer's Manual*. New York: C.M.Saxon, Barker & Co., 1860.

———. *Todd's Country Homes or Winning Solid Wealth*. Philadelphia: Hubbard Bros., 1888.

Vaux, Calvert. *Villas and Cottages*. New York: Harper & Brothers, 1857.

Wheeler, Gervase. *Rural Homes*. New York: Charles Scribner, 1851.

———. *Homes for the People in Suburb and Country*. New York: Charles Scribner, 1855.

Weld, Col. Mason C. ed. *Keeping One Cow*. New York: Orange Judd Co., 1880.

Woodward, George E. *Woodward's Country Homes*. New York: George E. & F.W. Woodward, 1865.

———. *Woodward's Architecture, Landscape Gardening and Rural Art, No. I*. New York: George E. & F.W.Woodward, 1866.

———. *Woodward's Architecture and Rural Art, No. II*. New York: George E. Woodward, 1867.

———. *Woodward's Cottages and Farmhouses*. New York: The American News Company, 1867.

——— and Edward G. Thompson. *Woodward's National Architect*. New York: George E. Woodward, 1868.

19th Century Magazines, Almanacs and Farm Journals

The American Agriculturist.

The American Magazine.

Arthur's Ladies' Magazine.

The Breeder's Gazette.

Carpentry & Building.

The Country Gentleman.

The Cultivator.

Genessee Farmer.

Godey's Lady's Book.

Harper's New Monthly Magazine.

The Homestead.

The Horticulturist.

The New England Farmer.

Ohio Farmer.

Peal's Popular Educator.

Peterson's Magazine.

Prairie Farmer.

The Register of Rural Affairs.

The Rural American.

The Rural New Yorker.

The Southern Cultivator.

Vick's Magazine.

INDEX